My DEAREST CINDY:

I bought this book, I must confess, for both of us. I have my problems but ~~~ you. The reason the book ~~~ is that we are so good ~~~ even spreading them arou~~~ got to know how much you mean to me. You are my own true friend, I have no real others. You are my best half of my soul, I separate you at no time from my thoughts. You are inseparable as I think of the past and future.

When you ride your broom we all get to ride. Of late I have been walking on the edge. I cannot walk the edge and ride the broom with you and also keep my balance.

I bought this to help you and I to keep our balance. Please love me and hang on to me.

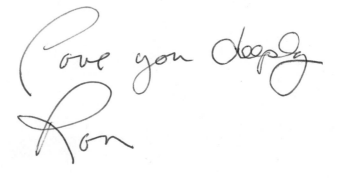

Love you deeply
Ron

# I Didn't Plan To Be A Witch

## A Guide
## for Frustrated Mothers
## Everywhere

By

Linda J. Eyre

## Other books by Linda J. Eyre

*A Joyful Mother of Children*
*Teaching Children Joy* *
*Teaching Children Responsibility* *
*Teaching Children Sensitivity* *
*Teaching Children Charity* *
*Lifebalance* *

*co-authored with Richard M. Eyre.*

*For the warlock*
*werewolves*
*and wee ones*
*living in our home —*
*with the hope that through the reading*
*they will understand...*
*and smile*

# Contents

# Preface

Every mother deserves a chance to communicate, contemplate and commiserate as she tackles the monumental task of raising children. My hope for this book is that it will provide that chance, along with a little relief for those who think they should be supermom but can't seem to pull it all together. Although some relief may come in the form of concrete suggestions, I hope that much will also come in the form of comic relief as the reader realizes that at least things are worse at the Eyres' house.

Because mothers have very little time to read, whether they are dealing with the physical strain of preschoolers or the emotional strains of adolescents, or both, the book is organized into thirty-one short chapters which can be read independently and in any order, according to the present need. It is written to mothers of children from toddlers to teenagers.

I always cringe when I hear that women without children or with just one sweet, little bundle who can't talk back yet have read this "real" stuff — for fear it will stunt their child-bearing capabilities. For them I hope it sounds fun as well as crazy!

The style is purposely conversational because I feel that I'm writing to my friends — that vast club of women called mothers, who rise above unthinkable odds in spite of their "witchhood" to be called by their children "the best mother in the world."

My special love and gratitude go to my children — to Saren, our oldest, who has done some of the editing for the manuscript, and to the other children who have been offered the right of censorship due any unsuspecting guinea pig. For them, I hope that there is not an invation of privacy, but a celebration of experience.

Love and appreciation also go to Richard, who encouraged every effort and saw that I had Wednesdays to write while he held down the fort.

Credit also goes to the tens of thousands of parents across the world who now belong to HOMEBASE,* our international co-op of families, and who participate in Joy Schools and the other programs based on our earlier books. So many good ideas have come to us from so many parents in so many places!

*See last pages of this book for information about HOMEBASE and The Joy Schools, TCR, TCC and Lifebalance programs.

# Spouse's Preface

After a parenting lecture that Linda and I gave recently, an attractive, bubbly young mother (the kind who says exactly what comes to mind without thinking too much about it) came up and, since Linda was occupied with someone else, approached me.

"Oh, Richard," she said, "Your books are so wonderful and theoretical. They just make me feel all overwhelmed and guilty inside — like I could never do it all."

I must have looked startled or hurt because she quickly tried again: "And tell Linda that I love her books; they're so funny and so realistic, and they make me feel like she's really there, and everything's OK. They make me feel so good because my problems aren't so different from everyone else's."

It's true. Linda has the rare gift of being gifted and good at so many things without arousing feelings of intimidation or jealousy. She has a remarkable quality that I call confident humility. She sees herself much more as a learner than a teacher. In our marriage, she is remarkably supportive, but she expects and demands, if necessary, equal support for herself from me. She has an independent, strong-willed feistiness that balances her humility and support. She fits perfectly Webster's second definition of a witch: a bewitching and fascinating woman.

Part of Linda's exceptional skill as a mother springs from her ability to remember what it was like to be a child and to empathize with our children. She also reminds me often that even though it seems like our children will always be around, they are actually only with us for perhaps a quarter or a third of our lives. We must experience and relish the relatively short time we have with them and make memories out of moments.

In 1982, when Linda was named by the National Council of Women as one of the six outstanding women under thirty-five in America, the other five recipients were an astronaut, a judge, a doctor, a publisher, and a corporate president. When the governor of New York presented Linda's award, he said it recognized "not so much her talents as a musician and a writer but her choice to make motherhood her highest career."

It behooves all of us, particularly us fathers and husbands, to remember that, while it is nice to say our wives support us, it really works the other way around. We support our wives! What happens outside the house takes place to support what happens inside the home.

As I write this preface, I'm sitting on my side of our "partners desk," looking across at Linda who is writing at her side of the desk. The thought comes, as it always does when I look at her, that I surely love my partner — even if people do like her books better than mine!

*Richard Eyre*

# Prologue

I should have known that being a mother wasn't going to be exactly as I'd dreamed it would be when I was in labor with our first child. By the time I hobbled into the hospital, my pains were not anything like our Lamaze classes had described. According to the books' calculations, I should be able to control the pain by breathing slowly and then more quickly, according to the intensity of the pain, to stay relaxed and comfortable without anesthesia.

On a one to ten scale, the incessant pains leapt from one to ten before I could even gasp, and stayed at the exquisite level for a full minute. If pain could kill, I was sure I would be gone.

"Give me anything you've got for pain, and lots of it!" I pleaded in a way that would have made my Lamaze teacher ashamed to say she knew me.

Not too much later the astonished nursing staff agreed that I was about to deliver a baby. They asked me to move from one stretcher to the next during the height of a contraction. This seemed about as logical to me as asking a prisoner of the Viet Cong to walk out and get the next prisoner just after having chopped off his feet.

On the delivery table, having cast modesty to the wind, I felt angry because none of the anesthesia had worked and absolutely terrified because I had finally fully realized, amidst the uncontrollable pains, that there was only one way out for this strange little individual who had been thrashing about inside the big bump for the past several months. Secretly I committed *never* to do this again.

Yet, something happened at the moment that gorgeous, bluish creature emerged into the real world and struggled for the first gasp of light and breath.

At that moment I emitted a sound which I have only been able to make nine times in my life. It indicates that the exquisite agony has been replaced with a more exquisite joy.

Everyone present, including Daddy and doctor, knew as they watched the tiny fingers and toes unfold that they had witnessed a miracle.

Nine times I could retell this exact story — with slight variations on the labors. (Twice the anesthesia worked.) During nine pregnancies I have felt the preoccupation with not being able to walk past a restroom door for nine months, not being able to see my feet, and not being able to get a decent night's rest without being disturbed by my twenty-five pound watermelon in motion. (Not to mention the pinched nerves, hemorrhoids, nausea, premature labor, and the battle of the bulge.) Nine times I have experienced the agony and the ecstacy of delivering beautiful children to this very interesting and complex world.

Just as I could never have known the realities of a pregnancy, labor and delivery, I could have never imagined the agony and the ecstasy of molding their incredible lives as they have shaped mine. I have become who I am, not in spite of these remarkably challenging individuals — but because of them.

# 1

# *I Didn't Plan To Be A Witch*

Before I had children, I envisioned what fun mothering would be: adorable, little children calling me "Mommy"; immaculate, beautiful, little girls skipping off to school in dresses I had sewn with my own hands; freckle-faced boys with lots of energy who made life exciting. Just thinking of seeing my children enacting a nativity scene at Christmastime brought a tear to my eye. Every day, but especially holidays, would be so much fun. Take Halloween for instance — I envisioned happy faces of children delighted with this night of make-believe and treats, complete with clever, carefully organized costumes.

I planned to be the best mother who ever lived! I would always bake cookies to welcome them home after school, and I would always lend a listening ear whenever a child had something to share. I would be patient, kind, positive, encouraging and most of all, loving — no matter what the situation.

Nine children later, I see things a little more realistically. The incredible complexities of the growing-up process never ceases to astound me. I still plan for the ideal: every day I attempt to remember that a soft answer turneth away wrath (Proverbs 15:1) and try to be the calm "eye" of the hurricane that passes so regularly through our household. And sometimes I succeed and am proud. But many times I have to shake my head in despair and think: "I didn't *plan* to be a witch!"

Let me illustrate with you just one day at the Eyre home. This particular day was the day before Halloween. Because I had been writing all morning to meet a deadline, I had let the house fall apart. A new neighbor across the street dropped by for the first time and slipped through orange pop and stuck to pomegranate juice on the kitchen floor while she told me she was searching for the kids who had shot her new yard lamps out with a BB gun twice!

I assured her that I did not even allow our children to have squirt guns hoping that she was too mad to notice leftover breakfast on the table and the paper shredding that our toddler, Eli, had entertained himself with a few minutes before.

At one o'clock Noah began saying he was sick, which would normally not be a crisis — except that he was having his three-year-old birthday party at three o'clock. By two o'clock, I had dressed Eli in his party clothes and, hoping for the best with Noah, loaded them both into the car to take some art prints, which were overdue, back to the library and to get some more for next month's PTA project. It was my last chance before leaving town for five days.

I really became worried when Noah refused a

hamburger on the way and lay down in the back seat, as pale as a Halloween ghost. Before we got out of the library, Noah had asked to lie down on all three floors as we traveled up the escalator.

"Noah, I think we'd better dash home and call and tell your friends to come tomorrow instead of today!" He immediately brightened and said he was feeling much better. He ate his hamburger all the way home and smiled every time I looked at him.

The party guests arrived promptly at 3:00, and I prayed that my husband had remembered to pick up our eighth grader, Shawni, and that he would soon be home to get the music book for Saren, our oldest, then pick her up at the high school to take her to her harp lesson by 3:30 p.m.

The phone rang, and the caller — the mother who was to pick up the elementary school children — had an emergency and asked if I could take her turn. I handed the cake knife to a mother whose three-year-old had not allowed her to leave and asked her to feed the kids while I dashed to the school for the dozen kids in the afternoon car pool.

While my husband drove Saren to her harp lesson and took Noah and his friends to the kiddie spook alley (including baby Eli, who was by now covered with ketchup), I tackled the next problems at home. Our fifth- and sixth-grade children had to have an old man's and an old lady's costume by 5:30 p.m. and were desperately begging to be taken to the thrift store.

We hurried off to find what we could, picked up Saren from her harp lesson, sent Jonah to Cub Scouts, and rushed home to get four other children ready for the Halloween party at the church. They each needed a costume and a piece of fruit to put in baskets for residents of the rest home they were visiting. Amidst telephone calls, chicken nuggets dowsed in honey (which joined the pomegranate juice and cereal on the kitchen floor), I

4/I Didn't Plan To Be A Witch

managed to get everyone out the door — but not without many tears and several costume changes. Two children forgot fruit, but I had sent an extra pear with an older child to give to the six-year-old who promptly ate it when it was handed to him. (I guess he didn't get any chicken nuggets.)

Meanwhile back at home, our 13-year-old was worrying about whether to go to her church party because she had so much homework and felt sure that none of her friends would be there. The 15-year-old was pushing me out to the car so that she could get to her play rehearsal on time, and I was trying to comfort Noah who had thrown up in the car during the final moments of his party. (Luckily, all the children were there watching so they could tell their mothers about the most exciting part of the birthday party.)

When the kids started filtering in from their party, one said he was in big trouble because he had ten reports due on Friday. When I asked him how long he'd known about it, he mumbled, "Only about three weeks." As I tried to help him get started, our fifth grader became exasperated because I wouldn't stop to tell her how to spell *horses*. (This is our fifth grader who still spells *mother* m-u-t-h-e-r.) Next the first grader announced with tears in his eyes that he left his costume in his teacher's car, and he had to have it for the Halloween parade in the morning.

Next, our 16-year-old rushed in and asked to take the car to her party and claimed that she'd love to help with the dishes but someone was waiting for her and was gone.

Within the next minute, our 13-year-old, who had returned from her party, told me that she'd invited a friend to sleep over so they could get ready for Halloween together the next day. She immediately began weeping and wailing when I told her that that was simply out of the question!

It was about right there that it happened! I got out

the well-used wart for my nose, my broom and my black hat and became a full-fledged, ranting and raving, bona fide witch!

"If you'd have thought for two minutes, you'd have known what a dumb idea that was!" (*Me* calling my child dumb! Not *me*!) "What were you going to do with your friend at 6:00 a.m. while you're practicing? What should I do with you tomorrow night when you have to finish a book report and you're crying because you can't keep your eyes open because you stayed up all night! I'll call your friend and tell her it was all a big mistake!"

When Josh asked for help with his social studies crossword puzzle, I snapped, "Go look it up in your book. I've got things to do, too." When Saydi came to tell me about the wonderful, new deal at Pizza Hut, I said, "Saydi, I can't talk now. It's past your bedtime. GET IN BED!" When Josh came back up the second time after his bedtime with a coupon to save us money, I yelled, "Josh, go downstairs to bed and *do not* come back up for any reason." As he stomped off down the stairs, I did shout, "Unless the house is on fire!" When Jonah came up a half hour after his bedtime to tell me that it was going to be too hard to be a limousine for Halloween (the costume he had planned for months) and since his friend wouldn't wear the wig to their matching clown costumes, he'd decided to be a karate guy for the Halloween parade and would I come and help him find an outfit, my eyes widened with rage and I yelled, "Jonah, if I see your face again before morning, I'm going to scream!" He also stomped off to bed and slammed the door.

Later that night, as usual after one of these hectic days, I looked back with relief that it was over and felt remorse that I didn't hold off being a witch just a little longer. I also realized how funny all those crazy events seemed when I looked back on them.

I did repent the next morning and explained to the kids that I'd been up since 5:00 a.m. and had had a hard day. Although they each only appreciated their own problems and couldn't know what it would be like to combine all those experiences, they forgave me.

No, mothering is not exactly what I had envisioned. The hard times are much more difficult than I could ever have predicted. But the good times are so much better than my wildest imaginings!

I do get tears in my eyes when I see my children perform in the Christmas nativity play, but I cry more because of what I believe they are feeling as they think about the real meaning of Christmas than because of how cute they are. My heart throbs when I see my little boys running off to school in their too-small, no-knees jeans helping each other with books and lunch boxes. I'd give anything to listen to a whole talk in church, *any* kind of talk, but I am thrilled beyond measure when those noisy, wiggly, sometimes irreverent, little cherubs share spiritual experiences with the family at the Sunday dinner table.

Yes, life is hard when relating to children and a husband, but no one ever progresses by passing from ease to ease! Buy a couch that can only be ruined by someone putting a knife through it and sure enough, one of the kids gets a knife and puts it right through it. When you *have* to be on time, someone always loses his shoes!

However, because of all the disasters we manage each day, we mothers have a magnificent opportunity to magnify our abilities and to master ourselves through the sheer volume of opportunities we experience each day. Without realizing it, we are practicing more every day than our children who are learning to play musical instruments. How well we think in advance and practice with the right goals in mind is the determining factor in what kind of mothers we become.

Many ideas for practicing and improving will appear in the following chapters. But I can almost guarantee that even with all our efforts, there will still be moments when we will get out black hats and brooms again and then afterwards shake our heads and say with discouragement, "I didn't plan to be a witch." Don't expect perfection but begin practicing your improvement. And remember that the very best thing you can say about yourself next year at this time is, "I'm getting a little better."

2

# A Stress Test

A friend called me from Maryland last week. Since she and her family had just moved, she told me about the kids' new schools, one son's new Suzuki lessons and how cute he was with his new violin, another child's insecurities, and another's successes. She also told me about the remodeling of their new home and that she was pregnant with their eighth child.

She said they had had several house guests and many social commitments in conjunction with her husband's new job as the chief executive officer of a large corporation. "Everything is going very well," she said, "except for one thing: I can't sleep."

Night after night she was lying awake, not being

able to sleep and not knowing why. "I guess it might have something to do with the pregnancy," she explained, "but it started before I was pregnant. I don't really feel worried about anything specific when I go to bed. I just can't figure it out!"

After I repeated back to her the things she had just told me, we both agreed that her insomnia had to be stress-related! Often as we take on one thing at a time, the load increases so gradually that we hardly know it is getting heavier. Unfortunately, sometimes it can get so heavy that one more added responsibility can break a mother's back.

After her call, I sat down and quickly (and easily, through experience) jotted down many things that could cause stress in our lives. I realize some things cause more stress to some women than they do to others.

Try taking this very unscientific stress test, judging the stress each item causes you on a scale from zero to ten: zero being no stress and ten representing the highest stress. Add your own stressful items in the spaces provided if you don't find them on the list.

**Stress Test**

(0-10 points)
1. Sleep (not getting enough and its effect on your performance)
2. Exercise (lack of it or guilt feelings because you know you should)
3. Diet (guilt feelings because of your weight or irritability because you're dieting)
4. Pregnancy (hormones and health problems because you are or guilt feelings or frustration because you're not)
5. Nursing a baby (schedule restraints or having not enough or too much milk)
6. Number of children (count one point for each

child — preschoolers and teenagers count double. This score may add up to more than 10.)

7. Working outside the home (guilt feelings for leaving or time and emotional demands because of)
8. Relationship with husband (personality and/ or sexual incompatibility)
9. Church involvement (feelings of not doing enough or doing too much)
10. PTA or school involvement (feelings of not doing enough or doing too much)
11. Social engagements (job-related commitments or too few or too many engagements with friends)
12. Financial needs (disagreement with husband over or worries, frustrations, and difficulties with)
13. Time (not having enough time or frustration in managing time)
14. Size of house (too small — no place to put anything or too large — taking too much time to keep up)
15. Guests in home (frequency of and entertaining, food preparation, house preparation)
16. Lessons (from soccer to piano — count double points for lessons that require your help during the week, i.e., sitting with beginners for practice)
17. Car pools (to and from school, lessons, church activities, field trips)
18. Homework and children's grades (too much help required from you or feelings that you don't help enough or pressure to produce good students)
19. Parents and parents-in-law (health problems or difficult relationship with)

20. Sibling rivalry (referee tactics inadequate or emotional wear and tear because of)
21. Family responsibility (single-parent stress, martyr syndrome, or need to teach children to help)
22. Order (amount of clutter or lack of cooperation to control)
23. Obedience (struggle with the balance between control and free agency)
24. Babysitting (frustration over finding one, using one too often, or not being able to afford one)
25. Cooking (meal preparation or concern over nutrition and variety)
26. Laundry (amount of or inability to find matched socks)
27. Tone of voice (household often angry or you are stressed and up-tight)
28. Health (general well-being, health problems, depression or fear of disease)
29. Children's friends (or concern about child's lack of friends)
30. Cleaning (lack of help with or ability to accomplish)
31. Change (a recent move or new job or feeling the need to change behavior)
32. Shopping (confusion of shopping for groceries with preschoolers or not having time or money or good judgment to get what you need)
33. Monthly periods (accompanying emotional ups and downs, as well as actually feeling ill)
34. Car and appliance break-downs (frequency of or inconvenience and cost of)
35. Teenagers (dating, driving, or defiance)
36. Lack of creative outlets (not having time to do your own thing or feeling the martyr syndrome, etc.)

37. Conflicts with a boss or people at work (intensity of or frequency of)
38. Husband's job (time demands or lack of promotion, etc.)
39. Friends and neighbors (conflicts with or lack of involvement with)
40. Arguments (with husband and/or children or other family members)
41.

42.

43.

44.

45.

Now go back over the test and see where most of your stress lies. There is often a pattern of stress in our lives. In giving this test to hundreds of mothers (who have also helped me compile the list), I have found that there is no scientific way to score this test. Feeling great stress over only one item on the list is enough for you to feel out of control. However, I have found that many women feel better about handling their stress just because they have discovered so many good reasons for it!

Having pinpointed some of the greatest causes of stress in your life, use your mental energy to help you devise some ways to reduce your stress level. After you have discovered as many as you can, see if some of the suggestions in the following chapters offer additional help.

*3*

# The Key: Simplify, Simplify, Simplify

I am convinced that the single, best, all-purpose answer to cutting stress in your life is learning to simplify. The other day while watching seven-year-old Talmadge's new gerbil running frantically around his treadwheel, I realized that I often feel exactly like that gerbil, running frantically from place to place, trying to get everything done, and ending up right back where I started the next day. When people say to me, "How do you do it all?" the answer is simple: "I don't! I just try to simplify." I love Emerson's quote: "Our lives are frittered away by detail. Simplify, Simplify."

The following are some ideas for simplifying that have worked for me. Keep in mind that I am simplifying with nine children of varying ages. Ignore the suggestions that don't apply to you; then think of your own methods according to your circumstances and the things you have just learned about yourself through taking the stress test.

1. *Learn to prioritize from moment to moment.* When you write down your schedule for the day, try to follow it, but if something more important comes up, don't hesistate to disregard it and do the more important thing. Realize that a few things are really worth doing, so they should be done well. Most of these things have to do with your relationship with your husband, children, and family. Remember that relationships, especially those with family members, are infinitely more important than achievements and that many special moments usually only come once. Some things are sort of worth doing, so do them sort of well. For me, this includes things like having a nice meal that requires extra effort once a week, or presenting a class on "Halloween ideas." Other things like making elaborate posters or cakes for the sake of good impressions are hardly worth doing at all. Coin a new phrase: If something is just barely worth doing, then just barely do it!

2. *Set time limits for routine tasks.* For those deathly boring and routine tasks such as clearing the kitchen in the morning or doing the laundry, push yourself to hurry. You can get twice as much done if you pretend you're in a race. Set a time limit and then *stop.* I could spend 24 hours every day just clearing clutter and doing the laundry. I could spend even more time if I worried about corners and dust. If having the clutter in the kitchen cleared really helps your mind and helps you function better during the day, do it first. Remember: "thing order" precedes "thought order." If you have to work outside the home, your time limit is set for you, which sometimes is a great advantage. A mother's work is never done if you think you always have to do all there is to do. Put on good music while you work. I like classical music

because it gives me ideas.

The hardest part is quitting. If I come to the end of my time limit and the three-year-old's bed isn't made and he's gone to nursery school or to play with a friend, I've learned to say to myself what I've scorned the children saying all their lives, "Oh, well, he'll just be sleeping in it again tonight anyway!" Then I close the door and make a mental note not to go back into that room until bedtime.

3. *Be flexible.* If something unexpected occurs, don't fall apart. Be willing to adjust your plans, and don't fret about what you've had to change. I have a husband who unplans many things that I plan. Sometimes I get all the children ready for a weekend trip to Grandma's, and we are all standing on the porch with sleeping bags when he comes home and breaks the news that something very crucial has come up and we won't be able to go until the next day. Our family is getting to the point that we all look at each other and say in unison, "One thing you have to be when you live with Daddy is flexible." (He insists that it is a foolish man who never changes his mind.)

Certainly there are times when what you have planned is really more important than the alternative plan, but being flexible in most cases simplifies your life.

Let the teenagers wear what they want to unless it's actually immodest or immoral. Put the baby down for a nap a little later if an opportunity arises to help someone during nap time. If a family crisis occurs on a day when you've planned a nice meal, call out for pizza. The flexibility list is endless.

4. *Encourage the older children to take some responsibility for the younger ones.* Our family has a tutor-tutee system that simplifies things immensely. The children over eight are called tutors (much to their delight) and the little ones are tutees. Every month each tutor is assigned a tutee whom he helps at dinner time, holds hands with at the zoo, gets pajamas on, tells stories to at bedtime, and is generally in charge of for that

month. For a family with several small children, this form of "middle management" is a great simplifier.

5. *Quit buying things you don't need.* We have a friend, the artistic director for the largest advertising agency in New York City, who insists that advertising is simply a way to make people believe that they need things that they actually only want. The Japanese have long known that "Simple is Beautiful," but Americans keep insisting that "More is Magnificent."

We need to change our thinking from "That's darling; I'll buy it" to "That's darling, but it's just another 'thing.' " Our lives are cluttered with "things." One of the best actions we can take to simplify our lives is to get rid of excess things that have to be dusted, cleaned, or picked up. De-clutter your house! At least once a year I try to go through closets and drawers at the rate of about one per day. If the items there have not been actively used since I last cleaned I tell myself that someone should be using it and promptly give it to the nearest charitable organization.*

6. *Consolidate errands and eliminate the ones that are only busy work.* On my way home from driving the car pool to school, I will often stop at the bank, pick up clothing from the cleaners, and do my weekly grocery shopping rather than make an extra trip during the day to accomplish these errands.

7. *Ignore outrageous statements by teenagers.* Eke out a frozen smile, if possible, and try not to argue. Teenagers don't usually mean it anyway. If their particular request is not immoral, illegal, or impossible, let them have their way whenever possible. One of the most amazing things I've learned about my teenagers is that they are actually the ones who are right at least half the time. Once a decision is theirs the consequences are theirs. It simplifies your life immensely not to be engaged

---

*For more complete ideas on de-cluttering see the chapter on Order in *Teaching Children Joy* or *Teaching Children Responsibility*.

in constant emotional debates.

8. *Learn to say no when necessary and yes when necessary.* Say no to a PTA job if it's just one more burden to add to an already impossible schedule or say yes to a PTA job if you really want to do it and you want to really know what's happening at your child's school.

9. *Quit worrying about what other people think about you.* Don't let others' opinions stucture your life whether it be the neighbors or your mother-in-law (and quit judging others while you're at it). No one can judge you fairly until they've "walked in your moccasins" and vice versa. Do the things you swore you'd never do even in an emergency. Take the boys to church in unmatched socks if there's no alternative. Forget what people will think.

10. *Get help with the household cleaning.* For many young couples, this just isn't possible. But many who think that they can't afford it, might need to think again. I will never drive a new car because I decided a few years ago that I would rather give the car payments to a cleaning lady. I hire a mother-daughter team who help me two-and-a-half hours once a week. Not everything gets done in that amount of time and most things look about the same a few hours after they leave, but it simplifies my life immensely! I know that the bathrooms have been cleaned once a week whether they look like it or not, and I don't take "mess-ups" by the children nearly as personally as I used to. If I clean up, and the kids mess it up, I'm irate. If the cleaning ladies clean up, and the kids mess it up, I'm removed. I love driving around in old, beat-up cars! My investment in cleaning ladies has been one of the best investments I have ever made. During the summer months and on extended family trips, the family is given total responsibility again, which is very valuable. All the children who are old enough learn to clean everything (bathrooms, windows, and floors). Of course, the children have daily and weekly jobs through-

out the year — the cleaning ladies are for my benefit, not theirs.

11. *Simplify meals by preparing dinner in the morning whenever possible.* I often do all-day meals in a slow cooker or prepare casseroles in the morning to be popped into the oven later in the day. I have found that it takes only half as much time to prepare dinner in the morning, even with preschoolers around, as it does to do it in the afternoon with car pool schedules, practicing, supervising homework, lessons to run to, and Cub Scout meetings to conduct. I frequently use paper plates and cups, calculating I come out financially ahead when I consider hot water, soap, and time. Don't feel guilty about using fast foods when you need to. Their occasional use cuts down on pressure and the "five-o'clock-frenzy." Having a child (whose job it is to set the table), set the breakfast table just before bedtime really helps in the morning, too.

12. *Do it now!* If you have spent hours, months, or years worrying about your weight, your bad feelings toward someone, or even little procrastinating things like calling to thank someone for a meal or a kindness, put it on your schedule and do something about it today! Those kinds of things can weigh you down and keep your mind burdened and heavy for so long that you can't remember anymore why you feel depressed.

13. *Quit feeling guilty!* If it is necessary for you to work outside the home, quit feeling guilty. If your kids' grades are not as good as you think they should be, do all you can to help them by talking with the teacher and improving homework habits, but then let the responsibility be the child's, not yours. When you make a mistake, apologize and forget it. When you back into somebody's car, get it fixed and don't torture yourself. There is no sense in agonizing over things that can't be changed. If you're overweight and have been starting your diet tomorrow for years, forget it for a year, and

love yourself for the things you can do.

14. *Learn to say "so what!"* So what if I'm late for the meeting. So what if dinner is not on time. So what if both the knees are gone in Joshua's only good pair of school pants. So what if Noah's face is dirty at the grocery store. Ask yourself, "Will this really matter in ten years?" If the answer is yes, then keep hounding your child to practice the piano (even though she leaves notes in the mailbox that say: "Dear Mrs. Eyre, I refuse to deliver the mail any longer until you let Saydi quit taking piano lessons. Signed, The Mailman."). If the answer is no, who will remember in ten years that you weren't there for that meeting or that you were late for a parent-teacher conference. Reduce your self-induced stress by saying "so what!"

15. *Use the toughest times to realize that the normal times aren't so bad.* Borrow four more children for a week and learn that your usual routine isn't as difficult as you thought. Your life will seem so simple when they leave!

16. *Abandon your schedule and be spontaneous once in a while.* Even if it looks irresponsible, do something crazy just for one of the kids or just for yourself. Those will be the moments the kids will remember. Invite your own kids to a family Halloween party. Put a casserole in a pumpkin and use another pumpkin to stir up some sort of witch's brew with a little dry ice. Smile at remarks like "Mother, what has come over you." Miss all the soccer games and slip away for an overnight stay and Saturday shopping with your teenage daughter. Do something uncharacteristic and crazy like read a book, watch Sesame Street with the kids or ride a horse. It will make you feel free (and simple).

Most of these sixteen ways to simplify are easy to say but hard to do. On the other hand, I guess you can get so lax that you throw pride to the wind. Luckily, our older girls are now the ones who see that the kids' socks match for church and that we have at least one civilized meal a week with real plates instead of paper ones.

My list of simplifiers works for me. Go back to the stress test now with your methods for simplifying and actually alleviate some of the stress in your life. There will be some things that you really cannot change, but there will be others that you can change. Simplifying is an ongoing process which never really ends, but it is one which helps in the everyday battle with stress!

_4_

# The Supermom Syndrome

I have known and admired a certain friend for years, but just the other day I heard a story about her that made me like her even more. Apparently, when she was a young mother with several children close together and came to her wit's end, she would retire to a closet and scream. She screamed and screamed and maybe even beat on the wall a little until it was all out of her system and then would come out, ready to try again.

One day her husband came home while she was "screaming in the closet" and panicked when he heard the commotion. Darting about the house frantically to find the source, he found his oldest daughter and blurted urgently, "What's wrong. What's happening?"

"Oh, it's okay, Dad," the daughter reported calmly with a wave of her arm. "It's just Mom screaming in the closet. She does it all the time."

Let's face it. We all have days like that, many of them, in our mothering careers. Mothering is physically demanding and emotionally wearing. The accumulated stress can be handled in many ways. The one just mentioned is certainly better than screaming at the kids, which is another alternative. Many times we can even handle a grueling day well, remaining calm and collected and thinking of the right thing to say at the right time, but not always, sometimes not even often.

As I have visited with many mothers, I have become concerned that so many think they should be a supermom: stronger than their mother-in-law, faster than a PTA president with eight kids, and able to make bread, feed a neighbor, and make all their kids' clothes in a single bound! When they lose their temper or forget a dentist appointment, they seem discouraged and start telling themselves that they can't do anything right.

They have the mistaken idea that everyone "has it all together" except them, that there is something they are doing that makes things go wrong. What a terrible misconception! Over many years in talking to myriads of wonderful mothers, I have never met a mother who thinks she has it all together. The Sunday smiles do not always reflect the impossible week! So join the club of mothers who struggle. (Please send me a letter if you are a supermom without problems so I can quit denying that you exist.)

We all have discouraging days, times when we would give anything to take back our words or to remake a decision. The most important difference, however, between a happy mother and an unhappy one is not so much that the happy mom is always doing things right but that she is accepting her mistakes, not as rocks to crush her, but as stepping stones to help her get across the fast-moving stream of parenting.

The key to recuperating from the Supermom Syndrome is to spend a quiet half hour once a week, possibly on Sunday, setting goals. Consciously setting specific goals for improving your relationship with your husband and children might be a good place to start. Even though everything may not work out just as you planned, your priorities are right! I love T.S. Eliot's statement: "Teach us to care and not to care. Teach us to sit still!"

Plan a little time to think and then think to plan the things that are really important as well as possible to achieve. In mothering goals, don't plan "not to get mad even once this week." Instead plan how to handle your anger in more positive ways.

Plan well, but in your planning, remember not to expect perfection. Figure on several crises each day; plan on frustration. I believe that the only true supermoms are those who learn from their mistakes and use them to progress. And sometimes even that's not possible. Some days you just have to retire to the closet and scream.

# 5

# What About The Child Who Fails — or Will Herman Ever Amount To Anything?

This is a good day to write this chapter because I am depressed! I'm not talking about the chemical or hormone imbalance kind of depression. (I am pregnant so I guess that accounts for some of it.) What I'm talking about is the kind of depression that comes from banging your head against the wall after trying every conceivable reward, bribe, and punishment in the book and a lot that aren't and still being unable to motivate a child to get things done—to perform according to reasonable expectations.

At the moment, Herman is my problem. (The name has been changed to protect the not-so-innocent.) It is Herman's job to empty the dishwasher, but the dishwasher is always full! Herman's siblings get 25 cents for every article of clothing of Herman's (or anyone else's) that they pick up and put away. The fine comes out of Herman's hard-earned money. Yet there is always a pile of clothing on the floor in front of his drawers. Herman gets paid according to how much he practices, how often he makes his bed and cleans his room, and how consistently he does his household job. Unfortunately, Herman is getting poorer every week.

Herman often forgets his homework—until the last minute. He has also been known to forget to take it back even when he gets it done. When his teacher asks him for his work, he honestly can't remember whether he did it or not! Since Herman has to buy his own clothes (thank goodness for birthdays and Christmas or this child would be absolutely destitute), he has a limited supply of clothing. This morning when he went to his room to get ready for school, he found his clothes had nearly all disappeared! And what he could find in his drawers was dirty! (He can't keep the hamper separated in his mind from his drawers.) Now, Herman has gone to school before in dirty clothes, out of absolute necessity, but these were unthinkable!

"You empty the dishwasher," I said when I saw his frantic face, "and I'll find you something to wear."

Five minutes later when he came downstairs to his room, I said, "Herman, it's your practice time, so throw on these sweatpants and this sweater and get to it!"

Having just turned twelve may have made Herman realize that he could no longer wear sweatpants with holes in the knees to school. He just couldn't. Amidst his tears and some very unflattering remarks from me, we found some new birthday pants, six inches too long, tucked them under, and pinned them with the last four straight pins in the house. (Safety pins are nonexistent five minutes after I buy a new package.)

Just then, the car pool arrived early, and all three

boys' hair looked like it had been blown dry while they were standing on their heads. As usual, every brush and comb in the house was gone, even the ones I'd tied to the bathroom sink. (It doesn't take long to untie a knot in an emergency.) In desperation, I grabbed the nearest toothbrush and toothbrushed the boys' hair as they shot out the door.

I put my head in my hands as they drove off and looked down to see the dishwasher—still full of dishes. It was good that Herman had already left!

"Maybe Herman is mentally deficient," I thought as I shook my head and mourned the clothes on the floor, the bed not made, the trumpet not touched.

I thought back to a conversation I'd had with my good friend Margaret, a mother of seven boys, living without a husband for the last six months while he began a new job in another state.

"Last week I got so exasperated with Jason, I thought I was going to die," she said. "He was late for a meeting at school and after dashing up the stairs screaming, 'Jason, Jason, we're late,' I found him sitting at his computer, working on an intriguing new program in his pajamas! Furious, I proceeded to yell at him all the way to the school. Jason didn't have a chance to get a word in edgewise as I raved about how he was never going to amount to anything if he didn't get his act together and get where he was supposed to be on time. I reached the height of my righteous indignation as Jason got out of the car at school with a discouraged look on his junior high face. Just as he was about to shut the door, little, three-year-old Anthony, who had been listening from the back seat, looked up at his big brother and yelled, 'Jason, I love you!'

"Tears came to my eyes and I felt like such a fool," she said. "If it hadn't been for sweet, little Anthony, Jason would have gone to school feeling stupid and unloved!"

I was shaken from my thoughts when the phone rang. It was Herman. "Mom, I forgot the crepe paper for Mrs. Ellison's birthday party," he announced very timidly. He'd forgotten it amidst the disaster of the morning. "I'll bring it right down," I said without the least hint of irritation in my voice, which I'm sure was a surprise to him.

As I hurried to get ready to leave, the only toothbrush I could find was the one I had brushed the boys' hair with. I couldn't find my purse which I had just a few minutes before absent-mindedly put somewhere. "If Herman is mentally deficient," I thought, "it's because he is related to me!"

As I drove to the school, I remembered that a few days before, Daddy had staged a little "half-way-through-the-pregnancy party for me by buying me a cute sweater (it was for a skinny person—but some day it'll fit) and a video (which I didn't have time to watch). It was a truly moving gesture. Late that night, after bedtime, Herman came to me with a little brown lunch bag folded over. "I'm sorry I couldn't find anything better for your half-way-through-the-pregnancy party, Mom, but this was the best I could do." In the bag was one of his new pencils and a pencil sharpener, which I had seen the day before amidst the mess under his bed! I hugged him and was sure at that moment that he was going to amount to something wonderful!

This morning as I handed Herman the crepe paper at school, I grabbed the hand that reached out for the package and said, "Herman, I love you. I really do—even if you didn't empty the dishwasher." (I couldn't resist that one little reminder.) He smiled sheepishly and ran into the school with a little grin on his face. Again I realized how much I loved that child and was horrified at how near I had come to squelching his self-esteem.

Ah, having just written this down makes me feel better and forces me to realize that:

1. Some days are just like that.

2. Children come with their own personalities. Some are freer spirits than others, and we have to recognize that. We should never give up teaching correct principles, but we should allow children to be themselves in "putting them to use." Progress takes more time for some children than others. Remember that even though some children seem to be living in another world, that world may be better than ours.

3. Writing down depressing or discouraging moments helps.

4. Self-esteem for both parent and child are delicate commodities and should be analyzed and handled with gentle, loving care and valued more than any task completed or goal accomplished.

5. When you get to the end of your rope, tie a knot and hang on!

6. The greatest progression comes through adversity—especially for mothers.

# 6

# *Sibling Rivalry: Dissonance and Harmony*

I recently heard a lesson on Johann Sebastian Bach, from which I gained an insight I feel is useful to every mother who has children old enough to create dissonance. (That includes about all of us in one way or another.) I learned that Bach was really the great pioneer in the use of harmony, or several notes played together simultaneously to create a beautiful sound. Until Bach's time, most music had either been written with a one-line melody or with two melodies played simultaneously known as counterpoint.

Bach was a genius at putting together chords and establishing new rules to create complex, rich music. Bach used many methods to make his compositions moving and creative, one of which was *dissonance*. Over and over again, through passing tones and intentional "wrong" notes, he created a brief, uneasy feeling. Most interesting of all was the relief he could make the listener feel through the *resolution* of the dissonance.

Bach was a master at resolving the dissonance in his music in wonderful ways—sometimes in predictable ways; other times in creative, new ways. A man known for his "well-tempered clavichord," Bach spent a lifetime establishing music as "well-tempered."

So also should be our own households. I hope you heave a sigh of relief as you realize that dissonance is necessary to contrast with and resolve into harmony. Dissonance actually makes life more interesting. It helps us grow and progress. The important thing is how we resolve the dissonance. If we do it right, a feeling of even more harmony results, whereas the wrong resolution can cause even greater feelings of anxiety.

Think of a recent example of dissonance in your home and decide whether the dissonance was resolved to create harmony or more dissonance.

As you read the following example from our house, notice that it sometimes takes a little compromise and accommodation to turn dissonance into harmony:

I shouldn't have been surprised when eight-year-old Saydi asked if her friend could sleep overnight again this weekend, but I blurted out the resolution without reservation! "No way!" I said very emphatically while hurrying to finish the dishes so I wouldn't have to spend all morning in the kitchen cleaning up after the kids left for school.

"Why not?" she pleaded.

"You had Amy over last weekend. You stayed up all night, kept your sister awake with your giggling, and were a grizzly bear all the next day. I'm amazed that you would even dare ask."

"But Amy and I are best friends. We never get a

long chance to be together. Either she has a violin lesson after school or I have piano. I just don't see why we can't. Please, Mom, p-l-e-a-s-e!"

Saydi is your basic, great actress. Her pleading voice took on a sense of urgency, pain, panic. "I have to have a sleepover," she wailed as tears began plopping off her cheeks like a leaky faucet.

But I remembered my resolve from last week. "Absolutely not," I responded coldly. "I don't want to hear any more about it! Go do your practicing!"

With a fiery exit she yelled on her way down the stairs, hoping I would and wouldn't hear her at the same moment, "I never knew you could be so mean!"

As the "feathers settled," I knew I had made the right decision, but I just didn't feel right about it. There was a distinct discomfort lingering in the air. I realized that my method of resolution was not good. Deciding to look at the world through her eyes for a few minutes, I thought about how much she wanted to be with her friend. That little friend was someone who didn't demand anything from Saydi or judge her, who didn't make her feel like a little sister or expect her to be perfect. Maybe she did need her—but not all night.

Just as the children were ready to walk out the door for school, I called Saydi aside. "Why don't we have Amy come over after school and play and have dinner with us and then play again. That would give you girls lots of time to be together. Then about 7:30 p.m., we'll take her home so you can both get a good night's rest. How does that sound?"

After a big unsolicited kiss and hug, she skipped off to school looking as though the weight of the world had been lifted from her shoulders: a much happier resolution resulting in even greater harmony.

Dissonance is a part of life. Whether it's only a passing note or a big, out-of-shape chord, we need to expect it, even anticipate it, and sometimes think about resolutions in advance. Other times, we just need to keep working at it until it feels right. Remember: Interesting dissonance makes a greater harmony!

I wish I could say that we have found the great, golden key to stopping sibling rivalry forever at our house, but I can't. I've decided that sibling rivalry in various stages of intensity is part of living in a household which has more than one child.

Last night on a three-hour trip in the van, I decided to make a list of all the rivalry that occurred during the journey home. It was late, and all ten kids (our nine plus a friend) were tired. For one fleeting moment I worried that they would just all go to sleep and leave me without any good material. What a joke!

We started out with little things like, "Jonah is pinching me through the crack in the seat," and "Move your foot, Saren. It's in my hair." By the end of the journey, we had had one major battle between an eleven-year-old and two teenagers. The younger girl swore that they had awakened her on purpose, and the older girls were pleading innocence but insisted that she deserved to be awakened because she was taking all the room. Another scream emerged from the back as Josh wailed that his eyeball was scratched because Shawni had kicked him with her shoe. The dramatics of it all were amazing. I quit keeping track after the first ten rivalries and decided to simply summarize.

On the day-to-day basis, despite the fact that it doesn't stop sibling rivalry, we have found several things that help—some more with some children than with others.

First, when two children engage in a verbal battle, they are requested to sit on a couch together in a certain spot in our house and remain there until they are prepared to report what *they* did wrong. Of course, it's very easy for a child to know what the *other* child did wrong. If they get tired of sitting or can't figure out what they did wrong, they ask the other child to tell them what they did wrong so that they can resume their activities. We try to emphasize that "it takes two to tangle" and that even those who plead complete innocence need to realize that it was partly their fault, too.

Next, when hitting, biting, scratching, or other forms of mutilation occur, sometimes we feel that one sharp spank on the bottom (for the very young children) or isolation for a certain amount of time does wonders. We have found that the punishment really depends on the child. Two of our children love to be spanked—although they wouldn't admit it. They feel cleansed and ready to start anew. Two others are devastated by it and cannot get over it. Isolation works better for them. Most often, however, we like to give the children a chance to repent. If the child can say, "I'm sorry. Will you forgive me? I'll never do it again!" with sincerity, and then if the fighters can give each other a hug, the punishment is suspended. Somehow that little exchange of words and the physical touching always works wonders. (Maybe they're pretty good at it because they get so much practice!)

The principle that helps our family handle sibling rivalry most is to talk a lot about "What would Jesus do?" Whether or not you are Christian, you will have to agree that Jesus' personality was totally non-combative. He always returned good for evil, love for hatred, compassion for intolerance.

Often after our children are involved in an argument, we ask the children to role play the argument again and this time to try to think what Jesus would do: i.e., return a hug for a hit, an "I love you" for an "I hate you," etc. Although this seems to be the hardest lesson in life to learn, it can also be the most valuable one. Let us warn you, however, that it often takes years to sink in.

Even with all these approaches, the sibling rivalry at our house goes on and will undoubtedly continue for years. Maybe the biggest challenge to making the quarrels and arguments something to smile about in years hence, is to learn to control ourselves during these highly intense times so that we can direct the children without becoming involved!

The last suggestion is the hardest of all for us strong-willed Eyre parents to follow and that is to be a good example. As parents we should either try to settle our arguments out of earshot or else be sure that the arguments the children hear are handled like debates and that the children see a satisfactory resolution as well as the confrontation.

May we all keep reminding ourselves how much fun we're having, even through the smoke and fire!

# 7

# Changing "I-Have-To" to "I-Choose-To"

It had seemed that there were so many things I had to do in my life. One day last week chosen at random illustrates my predicament:

At 6:00 a.m. I rolled out of bed to help Shawni, whose day it was for special help on the piano because of a lesson the next day. By 6:30 a.m., two children were up and ready for our morning devotional (by ready, I mean curled up in a blanket on a living room chair—eyes glazed and bleary) so I hurried to waken the other two, one who sleeps with the baby and can't use an alarm clock and one whose alarm clock has been blaring obnoxiously for several minutes. Once the five oldest children were assembled, we spent a few minutes reading scriptures, memorizing a short saying, and praying together.

Then life began to get complicated. One child started fixing breakfast while four of us practiced a simplified Teleman string quartet for 15 minutes.

At 7:00 a.m. the child, who in my mind is hopelessly non-musical, needed help. Help only lasted for a few minutes, however, as I glanced at my watch and realized that breakfast must be on by 7:30 a.m. to get everyone where they needed to be on time. (The oldest had already made her own breakfast and left.)

I sent the child making breakfast (which he loves to do) to get dressed and clean his room (which he hates to do), finished preparing breakfast and rang the breakfast bell. Then I nagged the children to sit down and eat so they could finish their morning chores before school.

From then until school time, it was a matter of finding a brush, getting kids to do their morning jobs so that the table gets cleared and the floor swept before they leave (which is much easier to do myself), calling the Cub Scouts to remind them to bring hammers to den meeting, writing notes explaining why Josh lost his homework and that Saydi must be excused for a dentist appointment, as well as writing out a check for lunches because Talmadge was three dollars behind.

We jumped into the van at 8:25 a.m. and picked up the morning car pool. While at the school, I dropped off punch ingredients for the PTA Teacher Appreciation Week, totally aware that combing my hair at the stoplights really didn't help me look ready for the day and vaguely remembering a poll I saw last week in *U.S.A. Today* which said the average female Yuppie spends one hour and seventeen minutes per day getting herself ready!

Rushing home, I remembered that I had left clothes in the washer day before yesterday and that I still had to finish preparing for Joy School (a co-op nursery school), which was going to be at my house that morning, as well as clear a path to the toy room before the preschoolers arrived at 9:30 a.m. On the way home, I stopped at the store to pick up materials for the art activity and spent the next 30 minutes with last-minute preparations while thinking "I really don't have time for this."

I spent the next two and one-half hours teaching Joy School, being amazed at the children's creativity and being glad I had spent the time to do something that really mattered.

After Joy School, the moment the last child's mother arrived, I got in the car with my two preschoolers to pick up Saydi for her dentist appointment. After that appointment, I made a mad dash back to the school to drop off Saydi and then ran home to take care of the babysitting co-op children for a couple of hours, which would enable me to leave my children at one of their homes the next day for a couple of hours so that I could finish things at the office.

While I was babysitting, I rewashed the smelly wash and tried to find a few socks that resembled each other closely enough to be called pairs and cleaned up the broken milk bottle the boys thought they had cleaned up before school. I also noticed that there was a dead fish in the aquarium and that the gerbil cage smelled terrible!

At 2:50 p.m. I was back on the road with the preschoolers to pick one child up at one school and take her to work, then to pick up another one at the high school and drop her off at a harp lesson while I went back to pick up the elementary school car pool and then went back to the harp lesson to drop that child off to teach a music lesson at someone else's home.

The afternoon had disappeared, and it was 4:45 p.m. so I rushed home to throw on a "well-planned, well-prepared" dinner (consisting of fish fingers, macaroni and cheese, and peas) which had to be finished by 6:15 p.m. in order for the older children to fulfill their evening commitments, which I won't go into!

Almost daily I have felt overwhelmed by all of the things I have to do. But last week I relearned an old lesson in a new way. On Friday, we picked up a new member of our family at the airport. She had come directly that day from Shanghai, China. At age 22, she was away from her family for the first time in her life. The following three days with her were amazing to me.

We were delighted to see her enjoy her first hamburger, which she had thought would be ham and eggs between two pieces of bread, to watch her surprise at being able to drive on the grounds of the university campus, where she will be studying, without having to go through a security-controlled gate.

It was intriguing to learn that she and her parents, who translate in several languages fluently, live in a three-room home. "When I want to study, I go to the bathroom," she said. "We share our living room with another family."

The children were delighted to show her how to get into an American bed properly and explain how to take a hot shower. She was amazed at the VCR, the dishwasher, the microwave, the garbage disposal, and the washer and dryer.

On our first trip to the grocery store, everything looked so big and strange to her, and she wondered whether the daffodils were to look at or eat. She simply could not believe the volume of groceries we bought. (But then I guess most average-sized families can't either.)

We took turns at being amazed as we listened to her play the piano—the classics—Beethoven, Schubert and Mozart—after having taken piano lessons for only two years with no piano in her home. (She rode her bike 15 minutes each way to her teacher's or to a friend's home to practice.)

Most astounding was to hear her answer questions about life in her country. When we asked about family size, she told us that within the last few years the government had limited family size to one child per family. Government ostracism and heavy fines were imposed on parents who had additional children. We found that students were assigned an occupation according to their test scores and that she had been assigned early childhood education. We learned that mothers are allowed to stay home with their children for only one year after birth. They are then required to return to the factory where they must deliver their babies to factory nurseries.

Suddenly, as I looked back on my harried week of things I had to do just before she arrived, I saw them in a different light. What I had thought of as being "I-have-to's" were actually "I-choose-to's," and how grateful I was for them!

I did choose to have a large family.

I did choose to educate our children at home in their preschool years and as they got older, to run them all over town for lessons until it is ridiculous. (And they can choose what they want to become. Whether or not they achieve will depend on how determined they are.) I did choose to feed twelve people every day and to subject myself to the complexities of my life in general.

With our young friend's alternate lifestyle so close to me, suddenly I felt grateful for every discomfort and hassle and worry because I chose to have them. Although I know I will probably complain again and that I'll still be exhausted at the end of a day of "I-choose-to's," I can see—with clear, American vision—that I love my problems! And so should we all!

# 8

---

# They Told Me So: Finding Time to Read Aloud

One summer we had the wonderful opportunity of spending a month in the wilderness of Eastern Oregon building a log cabin from scratch. Despite dirt so thick that you would never have recognized any of us, scrapes, slivers, crushed hands and toes, and insect bites, it was one of the most interesting experiences we've ever had.

I could write another book concerning the wonders of life in the forest, the things we learned about the balance of nature, and how interesting it is to live without plumbing and electricity for a month. But for now, I'll confine my comments to something I learned that I didn't expect to learn and that people have been urging me to learn for years!

Every night, just before dusk, after dinner had been cooked on the open fire and the dishes had been washed and rinsed in hand-heated water, we put the little boys in bed and gathered around the campfire—sometimes to sing or tell stories, but most often to read aloud. When the eating and work and nature walks were done for the day, there was absolutely nothing left to do but read, which we all discovered we loved more than we could have possibly dreamed.

Oh sure, we had read books together sporadically before, but soon became exasperated by the telephone, the arrival of friends, or the little boys whining and fighting under our feet. Our reading had mostly been confined to summer when almost everybody slept in the same room anyway and usually Daddy would read until everyone dropped off. But I had seldom found much time to read aloud to my older children.

I had adamantly believed in reading to children and had been told and had read over and over how important it was: how much it helped your child's IQ and listening ability and vocabulary. I knew the benefits, but it took getting away from all the distractions—which were not more important, but were more pressing—for me to fully experience them.

After the first few chapters of Walter Furley's *The Island Stallion,* the girls, who had professed to being "bored silly with those dumb horse books," sneaked off to their tent one afternoon and read it aloud to each other, absolutely unable to wait until the next night to find out what happened next!

I found benefits far beyond all those I had read and believed in. Our six-year-old, shy and always staying in the background, loved to sit on my lap and be snuggled while I read. Our eight-year-old, while seeming to be preoccupied with other things in the beginning, began becoming visibly enthralled in the story. The most amazing transformation of all was found in our 11-year-old, who up to this point had no use for any books except encyclopedias and had to be forced to read just enough to eke out the required number of book reports each term.

He became obsessed with reading. All day it was, "How much longer until we get to read? How many chapters can we do tonight? What do you think will happen next?"

After the fire danger became too great and we could no longer build a campfire, we started reading around the propane lantern in the teepee. He was the first one to get all the sleeping bags arranged and light the lantern so that we could read.

He became so hooked on reading that he finished reading aloud to the rest of us the book that we started just before we left, *James and the Giant Peach* by Roald Dahl, on the intercom of the van all the way home. Even with the microphone he had to almost scream because the air conditioning was broken and all the windows had to be opened in the 100-degree heat. But he never despaired. Sometimes he would stop for an hour and then plunge right back into it, without prompting or suggestion. Now that's devotion!

During the rest of the summer, although we were back among the distractors of computers, television, and friends, we read together several of the Newbery Award winners.

At the end of the summer, I found that we had discovered something very precious. The children and I had been places together that we could never have gone in any other way than through the wonderful world of reading aloud.

Things we saw often reminded us of places and people we knew through our reading experience, giving us a common bond, private jokes, a loving sense of togetherness that had come to us in no other way.

"They had told me so," but I had to find it out for myself. Of course, the challenge is keeping the habit going through the school year, which becomes so hectic. I've told myself to put my priorities in order and keep reading aloud an important part of our family life. I'm convinced that it's possible, even if it's on a more limited scale, if the desire is there.

I strongly recommend your trying it too, if you haven't, and becoming more consistent if you have. Read *The Read Aloud Book* by Jim Trelease for motivation and wonderful ideas on what to read according to your children's age level and interests. Turn off the television and start reading together. It's a solid gold investment in time.

# 9

# *Walking the Tightrope of Uniqueness*

The age-old question over whether we gain our personalities through environment or heredity will probably never be fully resolved. My theory supposes "a little of each and a lot of neither."

One morning in the middle of my ninth pregnancy, with the help of an ultrasound scan, I watched a miracle. A tiny, new, little individual, who sprang into earthly existence only 21 weeks ago, moved suspended in her watery, weightless world and moved arms and legs freely. Hooked to an umbilical lifeline like an astronaut in space, we saw her face—her eyes, nose, and lips—like a black and white negative. She was totally unaware that we were watching, of course. It gave me chills to realize once again that somebody was in there. I am convinced that this new, little girl was already an individual—as unique and different from her brothers and sisters as they are from each other.

All eight of our children "on the outside world" are as different as the colors in the rainbow, all beautiful and complementary to each other (at times). We just think we have found the solution for one child's problems, and the next one comes along with the same problem but with a nature that needs to be handled in a totally different way.

This uniqueness manifests itself every day at our house. All the children work within the same boundaries called family laws. They all have jobs to do; they all accept responsibility—but in their own ways.

Two get up exactly when their alarms ring and are practicing right on time. One of those two is angry most of the morning and one is seldom ruffled by anything. Two others have to be literally dragged from their beds. One gets right to work as soon as she realizes she's awake, and the other manages to pass the next two-and-a-half hours doing absolutely nothing unless someone stands over him every waking moment.

Some are gifted in music. One started out being the worst violinist in the orchestra but progressed slowly, but surely, until she became first chair. Another almost effortlessly absorbs music but won't practice no matter what the bribe. Another couldn't play well if his life depended on it (for this year, anyway).

Some of our preschoolers have been curious about letters and shapes and colors; others couldn't see them even when they were pointed out. Very quiet ones listen for hours to those who cannot stop talking. Some get wonderful grades. One worries about grades unnecessarily while another usually waits to the very last second to come screeching in with knowledge and assignments. Still another can't remember if he studied for the test or not.

Even if he does his homework, he forgets to hand it in.

While some are rich with the money they have earned, others are penniless—even though both are presented with the same opportunities to earn money. The list could go on forever, and I'm sure that similar evidences apply in your house.

While this uniqueness is one of the most wonderful things to behold in our homes, it is also the thing that can turn us into instant witches, especially when we realize that we also have our own uniqueness to cope with as well as our husband's.

How do we walk the tightrope of uniqueness? How do we balance our uniqueness with the uniqueness of husband and children? Let's go back to music for a minute. How hard do we push children to practice? Do we push them whether they seem talented or not because it is a good discipline or because they may bloom later? Do they practice every day or only when we force them, only when we reward them, or only when they want to?

I have a friend who wants her children to be responsible and to be great musicians. (Incidentally, they are!) She calls practicing "milking the cows." The cows must be milked morning and night, day after day, month after month, year after year. Other mothers produce talented children by letting them practice when they want to—because they love it. (Not many children qualify for this type of music education, I might add.) Some mothers push so hard that children never touch their instruments again after they leave home. Some grown children scold their parents endlessly for not making them practice when they were too young to know what they wanted or needed.

I am sorry to say that I am not going to give answers or solutions for these complex matters. The answers lie with you and your uniqueness and depend on how much thought you give to the uniqueness of your children. Even at that, we will all probably still make mistakes.

We do need to keep two things in mind, however, as we analyze, sympathize, and tyrannize:

1. If our children do not keep pace with us—with our wants and desires for them, our needs and expectations—it may be because they "hear their own drummer." We need to allow them to develop in their own way, no matter how much we want them to develop in our way. We still must provide them with parameters for their own security, but children must have room to be individuals.

2. Children are not like clay—which we can mold into whatever we want if we try hard enough. They are seedlings. The seed of what they are has already been planted from the moment they began their existence. Some may be orange trees and others might be lemons. It is our job to observe, water, expose to the sun, weed, and nurture to make the most beautiful plant possible from the seedlings we are given.

3. Maybe the "other world" they are in is actually better than ours! We can learn a great deal from them if we will listen to them instead of insisting that they always do it our way.

# 10

# Looking at Motherhood Through Humor-tinted Glasses

One morning I stomped into the kitchen wearing my witch hat and broom while all the children were sitting at the breakfast table. I was already furious about how the day had gone thus far. Absolutely no one had done absolutely anything they were supposed to have done. No beds were made, no practicing was done; yet these chattering little "good-for-nothings" dared to be giggling at the breakfast table as though it were just another day!

Smoke must have been curling out of my ears as I, pregnant and hormone laden, began yelling at the kids—uncharacteristically loud and menacingly. "I can't believe what has happened this morning! Absolutely nothing! I

cannot believe that you have to have somebody screaming at you every minute in order to get anything done
around here," I raved. Some of the children looked
shocked; others amazed; one maybe even a little frightened.
But one with big, brown eyes and a grin on his face began
to giggle.

"Noah, don't you dare laugh at me when I'm this
angry. You're taking your life in your hands!" I screamed.
Seven-year-old Talmadge leaned his head over on sixteen-
year-old Saren's shoulder and began laughing, too. Suddenly I realized that it was as though someone had un-
corked some laughing gas. They were all tittering—just as
if they were watching a funny movie.

As the blinding truth finally sank in, I realized that
they were watching a funny movie, starring Me! Of
course, the only thing I could do was to grit my teeth, see
my ridiculousness, loosen up, and laugh with them.

Some days are definitely funnier than others!
Often our family's funniest days are on the Sundays after
I've been gone all day Saturday and haven't been able to
follow through in making sure the children lay out Sunday clothes and take baths.

A few clips of conversation which occurred one
Sunday morning will give you the picture:

Saydi (in tears): "Shawni tore two buttons off of
my dress."

Mom (exasperated): "Shawni, why did you do
that, for goodness sake?"

Shawni (feeling guilty): "I told her to clean up a
hundred times, and she just wouldn't do it! Finally, I
grabbed her by the back of the dress, and they just popped
off!"

Jonah (wailing): "Josh said the sign I made was
dumb!"

Mom (disappointed): "Remember the talk we had
about hurting others' feelings?"

Josh (combative): "Well he said my things were

dumb, too!''

Mom (gritting teeth): "Remember the talk we had about 'what Jesus would do?' "

Saren (frantic): "Mom, I forgot that I was supposed to play a violin piece for opening exercises. What should I play? Can you play the piano for me?"

Mom (wildly frustrated): "Saren, I am supposed to be in a special skit today at the same time you are supposed to be playing, and the baby has taken the script out of my desk. It's gone!"

Josh (carrying his only Sunday pants by two fingers and whining): "Mom, the cat wet on my pants!"

Mom (absolutely furious): "Josh, I told you not to put those pants on the floor by the litterbox. Put them in the washing machine and get them ready for church."

Shawni (turning from side to side in the mirror): "Mom, is this dressy enough?"

Saren (disgusted): "Mom, I can't find any clothes for the baby—and one of his new shoes is gone."

Talmadge (whining): "Mom, I can't find my shoes, either! I think they're at Chad's." (He had already left one pair at my sister's and another pair at my mother's that week.)

Already five minutes late for church, we hurried out the door. I glanced back at the disaster behind me as the door closed. Already seething as we drove to church, I also noticed that Jonah had sneaked out without a bath, Shawni had on shoes with no socks, Saren had forgotten her stand for her violin music, I had forgotten my shawl for the skit, Talmadge was wearing moonboots, the baby had thrown up on his last clean outfit, and Josh's pants were still obviously very damp.

Mom (seeing red and yelling): "All right you guys. This is it! I don't care if it is Sunday! After church we're all going home and getting that house cleaned up if it takes making everybody work their fingers to the bone!"

That day, after I got through with my skit and got

Saren through her violin solo, I sat in Sunday School Class and got the giggles. The longer I thought about that crazy morning, the funnier it got. "In a few years we won't believe such an hysterical morning could ever happen," I thought. I secretly committed myself to write down the events of the morning as proof that it actually happened!

We all know that the old formula—crisis + time = humor—is true. In hindsight I'd like to add that the shorter the time element is, the better for everyone's mental health. Life in a crisis-ridden existence can certainly be funnier and much more enjoyable if we look at the world not through rose-colored glasses, but through humor-tinted glasses. Although it's not always possible, seeing the humor in a disaster can change our reactions in any situation from witchy to wonderful and from tense to terrific!

# 11

# *Let's Make a Deal*

I know there are children in the world who do things they don't want to do just because they know they should, but we don't have many of them.

One summer we could see that the kids had some valuable time on their hands and we were fortunate enough to have a tennis court and basketball hoop right next to where we lived at a lake-side cabin. Even though the children really wanted to learn to play tennis, it didn't come first on their priority list of the day's events until daddy thought of "The Deals." He thought of something that each of our tennis and basketball playing-age children really, *really* wanted. Each reward was different according to what that child wanted most. For some "The

Deal" involved money, for others it was an excursion with a friend. Each deal involved quite an extensive reward but the work involved in the attainment of the reward seemed almost impossible — at least to me.

"Josh will never be able to volley back and forth 50 times without a miss, it's just not possible," I cried in my encouraging way.

After three weeks they were getting up at 6:00 a.m. to start practicing and were obsessed with completing their goals. To my amazement, when one week of the summer was left (August 31st was the deadline) three out of five kids had accomplished their goals. The other two, with tears in eyes, managed to squeak through with their victory on the last day. We will probably never see happier children than those two on that day.

"That's bribery!" some might cry, as they see that we pay our children to practice on the long term and think of every imaginable form of persuasion on the short term to keep them interested and plugging along. If bribery is what you call it then I guess it is. But I believe that the world works on a system of rewards and sometimes adding a little artificial "kick" helps get a child to the real reward of fulfillment and natural consequences.

It's so difficult for kids to see the good in what we ask them to do that it can't be all bad to offer rewards to get them where they will want to be when they realize what life is all about.

Almost every mother has wondered how much farther to push a child on piano lessons. We say to ourselves, "If I push too hard, he'll end up hating music and never touch the piano again after he leaves our nest. While on the other hand if I don't push hard enough he'll haunt me as an adult with questions like, 'Mother, why didn't you make me practice?' " Often, thoughtful "deals" in regard to music practice can prevent going off the deep end on either side.

I am quick to admit that there are some children

that no bribe, reward or deal will phase and with those at our house, I've given up for a year and then tried again the next. With some children a little rest does wonders and with others, it makes them all the more committed to noncompliance.

This year, after trying everything imaginable to motivate him to keep his room clean, I've resorted to asking one child just to keep his door shut at all times and to keep his "stuff" far enough away from the door that nothing falls out at me when I open it. Our relationship was beginning to suffer and I decided that the memory of a forever nagging mother was not worth a clean room. Maybe I'll try again next year.

In the meantime, I've just come up with a "new deal" for our third grader who is struggling with reading: Thirty days of reading aloud outside of school time for fifteen minutes per day equals new high-top basketball shoes. Basketball is his greatest love and he needs them desperately. He finds it almost impossible to sit still longer than five minutes but I had him cut out a picture of those "dream shoes" and tape it to his bed. It might just work!

# 12

# This Christmas...
# Listen For The Bells

One of my favorite children's books is the Caldecott Award winner *The Polar Express* by Chris Van Allsberg. Without revealing all the details of the story, I will just say that to me the book suggests that most children can "hear the bells" of Santa's sleigh at Christmas because of their simple faith and receptivity to the Spirit of Christmas. On the other hand, adults are usually oblivious to the "bells" because the commercialism and hassle has drowned out the sound. In his subtle way, the author makes the sound of the bells represent the real meaning of Christmas.

One of my worst problems at Christmastime is not being able to hear the bells. Every Christmas I vow that

I'm going to get organized sooner by having all my presents bought by December 1. I commit myself to quit accepting assignments to take special treats to the fourth grade when I don't even have time to make Christmas cookies with my own children, and resolve that I'm going to quit worrying about what clever new things to take to the neighbors. None of which I did with much success.

I became especially alarmed last year when I heard several mothers with large families say, "I hate Christmas. It is really the low point of my year." I must admit that I have had that very thought cross my mind and I have felt myself becoming a "witch" at the very time I should have been an "angel." I know at those times that I need to sit back and listen for the bells.

A good friend who is single shared with us his way of "hearing the bells" last holiday season. As a single, with quite stable financial resources, he felt a strong need to help other single men who were less fortunate than he. He thought he'd like to invite a couple of homeless men from the transient shelter to have Christmas Eve dinner with him. When he got to the shelter, he looked over the many faces which seemed to lack hope and decided to invite them all. He and a girl friend prepared a turkey dinner with all the trimmings to share with these homeless men. His father, who thought he was crazy, said, "Well, Gordon, if you have to do this, for heaven's sake, don't put out your sterling." Gordon thought it over carefully and decided to put out his very best—the china, crystal, and sterling. When the time for the dinner party arrived, he had all forty-five men picked up in taxis and brought to his home where they enjoyed a delicious holiday meal. In addition, each man was encouraged to make one long-distance phone call to loved ones who may be concerned about him. When the party was over, there were many expressions of thanks but the one from the last man to leave was one Gordon said he will never forget. The man had been quite emotional all evening. He turned to Gordon just before he got into the taxi and, holding Gordon's face in his hands, looked into his eyes and said with tears spilling down his cheeks, "Now I know what Jesus looks like!"

It is so easy to let the seemingly urgent needs make our minds so cluttered and noisy that we don't have time to "hear the bells" at Christmas. We don't have time to think about what Christmas really means and what we want for our children at Christmastime—not dolls and trucks and clothes—but peace and love and service.

I had begun to feel that I was not in control of Christmas; Christmas was in control of me. I was on a merry-go-round that demanded toys and gifts for everyone. Dozens of people needed to know of our love through a clever or handmade gift, not to mention the food, family parties, church parties, friends' parties, and kids' Santa Claus lists. The list went on and on and made me tired just thinking of it.

Last Christmas, on my way from one important errand to the next, I had an argument with myself about whether or not to stop in and see our darling, 87-year-old adopted grandfather.

Through the Community Services Council we had learned that he needed some help and support. Even though at 87 he was able to quite capably take care of himself and the little house he had built with his own hands, his biggest problem was loneliness. His wife, who had never been able to bear children, had died 45 years ago. His nine siblings had all passed away and his only living relatives, who lived 60 miles away, were two nephews, aged 82 and 88.

Our children loved to visit him and hear him tell stories about his childhood and working days, and watch him as he proudly showed vast numbers of his water colors, carefully etched by his untrained hands on pieces of construction paper, which virtually wallpapered his walls.

The hardest part of coming was leaving. He was still telling us stories hours later while we were walking down the stairs to get in the car.

Even though I had a hundred other pressing things to do to get ready for Christmas that December 23rd, I forced myself to stop by and see how he was doing, although I knew it would be almost impossible to get away.

When I opened the door, the pungent odor of sickness smacked my nose. There was Royden, hunched on his favorite chair, unable to move. The next four hours were spent getting him to the car, one inch at a time, and then finding doctors who could diagnose his problem, counseling with them about the coming need for Royden to be placed in a rest home, filling prescriptions, and then buying juice and food to help the recovery process.

Though I thought I could spare only a few minutes four hours earlier, I felt wonderful with Royden on my arm as he tottered up his front walk at the end of the afternoon. I could certainly hear those Christmas bells as I tucked him back into his special chair and a voice in my head began softly, "When ye have done it unto the least of these…"

This Christmas listen for the bells. Watch for opportunities to really hear them even if it's just taking a moment to make the lady at the checkout stand feel good about herself or helping a child, lost in a department store, to find his mother.

The following are a few suggestions which you will have to tailor to your own situation, but which may help to calm enough of the Christmas noise to help you hear the bells:

1. Close your eyes and visualize what you want for your family at Christmastime. Dream about traditions that would make your Christmas more memorable and sort them out from the ones that make it a hassle. Be

brave enough to lovingly tell your parents that it's time to start your own Christmas traditions on Christmas Eve, Christmas morning, or whatever, instead of being at a huge family party—if that is what you really want.

2. Write down a list of all the things that you would like to do at Christmas. Then mark each one with a VI (very important), SI (sort of important), or TD (trivial details). Plan exactly when to do the VI's. Fit the SI's in if you can, and forget the TD's.

3. Have a brunch after the opening of the Christmas gifts on Christmas morning (something simple but nice) instead of spending the rest of the day preparing a huge Christmas dinner (unless that is your favorite thing about Christmas), and *you* play with the kids' toys or watch the football games all afternoon, too!

4. Realize that some Christmases are more elaborate than others depending on your financial situation and the arrival and disposition of new babies and two-year-olds. Enjoy the differences instead of begrudging them.

5. Instead of worrying about what to give to the person who has everything and trudging all over town to find something appropriate, give a priceless gift—something from your heart—a written tribute.

6. Learn how to say no gracefully but with firmness and conviction. Also, be ready to offer alternate suggestions, i.e., instead of making gingerbread houses for each of the kids in your Sunday School class, give them a candy cane and a little note of appreciation. Or better yet, take them to deliver goods to a needy family.

7. Limit kids' Santa Claus lists to one major gift (cruel parents). Let them realize that it is not their option to ask for everything their hearts desire. You can fill in things from Mom and Dad that you want them to have or can reasonably give them.

8. Shop early and wrap presents as soon as you purchase them so that you can enjoy the nativity play by

the children on Christmas Eve and ponder the real meaning of Christmas without being preoccupied with the drudgery of staying up all night to wrap gifts. Save the assembly of toys for older children who can help on Christmas morning. Part of the excitement can be putting it together.

9. Make it a tradition to do something truly service-oriented, instead of getting caught up in making new decorations for the tree every year. Ideas can range from taking dinner to the elderly to making a lovely Christmas for a needy family whose children will go without if you don't provide. Next year we plan to follow the example of neighbors who took their children to Mexico for Christmas. They had planned to sit in the sun, but when it rained for two days, they decided to go to the village orphanage and see what was needed. They had their most memorable Christmas as they bought gifts for each little child of the orphanage and personally presented them. They had made their own pact not to receive one single gift for themselves.

Hear the bells by putting your visualizations of a happy, stress-reduced Christmas into reality. Regardless of what the media and your friends and children tell you, you're in charge of Christmas at your house. By listening for the bells, you may give the real meaning back to Christmas.

# 13

# The Perpetual Practice of Patience

Almost the universal response when I tell people that I now have nine children is, "My, you must have a lot of patience!" A list of the few good attributes that I did have at the time I began having children definitely did not include patience.

It took many years of struggling with my need to be patient, along with my desire and ability to have patience, to realize a simple fact: Patience is a learned skill—just as playing the piano is a learned skill.

Many people say, "I'd love to learn to play the piano," but when it comes right down to it, many don't have enough desire to learn to spend hundreds of hours of practice necessary to learn well enough for it to be useful. So goes patience.

It is true that some are born with natural gifts for music or patience which makes things much easier, but most of us have to "slug it out." We must have a burning desire and then plan and visualize, work and practice until we actually become better "players."

It is easy for psychologists and philosophers and husbands to say, "change your habits, be patient and understanding and never raise your voice." But the intricacies involved in remaining calm as a mother are unimaginable unless you are a mother!

The last time I lost my patience, which was yesterday afternoon, I found the experience frustrating and embarrassing. At the beginning of a Cub Scout meeting, I received a long-distance call from someone who needed help. With a crying baby on my legs, I tried to talk on the telephone while the Cub Scouts used the newly cleaned couch for a trampoline. A pillow fight ensued (our couch includes about 20 pillows). After I finished the call, I found that the baby had found the artists' chalks and had scattered them on the floor upon which the Cubs had thrown pillows and were jumping and sliding. Green and black, oil-based chalk was all over our couch and new, light beige, wool carpet. Next our twelve-year-old, whom I had just taken to the junior high to find her lost English papers which she was frantic about, was whining about not being able to have an ice cream bar even though Josh just had one. Of course, my wrath was showered on Josh, who at that moment had descended to the bottom of the stairs. Half an hour earlier he had *promised*—after begging for five minutes for an ice cream bar and reluctantly (after three "nos") receiving consent—that he would not let anyone see him eating it.

Pointing my finger at him I said in a very loud, exasperated voice, "Josh, you may *never, never, never* again have an ice cream bar after school."

"But Mom," he began.

"Just don't ever ask me again," I raved on, not letting him say another word! "I told you this would happen. I knew it! Now everyone's begging for ice cream."

I drew in my breath to finish, and he managed to get a word in. "Mom, I just wanted to tell you that Matthew's mom is here with his things."

I died when I looked up with finger still pointed in wrath at Josh to see Matthew's mom smiling down at me! Red-faced, I blubbered around and tried to explain my actions as we both giggled a little amidst whoops of Cub Scouts (luckily she's a mother, too)! Nevertheless, I was embarrassed at doing exactly what I promised myself I would not do.

Having already confessed to witchhood several times, I know that my progress to patience is very slow. I do think it helps, however, to have the following guidelines in mind as we practice patience.

1. *Don't overvalue material things.* When you buy something new, predetermine that the chances are more than 50-50 that it will soon be dented, mashed, crushed, broken, written on, spilled on, or scratched! Although it's wise to caution children and to do all you can to preserve your nice things, there's no reason to be reduced to a screaming bundle of nerves over things. Feelings are more important.

2. *Visualize yourself as the "calm center of the storm."* Before you leave your bedroom in the morning, spend one minute meditating about the events of the day. I usually do this in the bathroom, although I did not meditate on the date of this previously described "storm." Realize that you'll be frequently walking into "hurricane" situations and determine that no matter what happens, you are going to remain "the eye," the calm center of the storm.

3. *Set reachable goals.* Instead of setting a goal of being patient with all of your children, try to concentrate on being calm with one child at a time, especially

the one who is most exasperating. There will still be times when you lose your patience, but be willing to forgive yourself. You're only human. Explain your anger to your children when you get mad at them; let them know you're human too!

4. *Don't lose your control when your child says, "That isn't fair!"* Calmly remind him that *life* isn't fair so he'd better get used to it. It's how we handle the "punches" that really counts.

5. *Analyze your impatience.* Chart your impatience for a week. Every time you get angry, write down why. You'll probably discover some interesting things. Maybe you consistently get angry because your two-year-old is a walking wave of destruction or your 10-year-old is always late or your 12-year-old still whines. Write down (a) what bothers you and (b) how you react to each situation. Next, realize that one of those two things has to change. Premeditate and practice a new response to irritating behavior. For example, say, "I'd like to help you feel good about being on time. How can I help?" instead of "The car pool's waiting again! I just can't believe that you can't put your shoes where they belong so that you won't always be late for school!" Being patient is hard work, but well worth the practice.

6. *Use a still voice of perfect mildness.* Christ set the example of calmness. His voice was one of stillness and perfect mildness. Whether you realize it or not, the tone of your voice sets the mood for your household. Try a fun experiment. Memorize the following statement: "Overwhelm them with calmness." It's a mental concept that can be brought about physically sometimes.

Even as I review these guidelines, I find that I still lash out at an unsuspecting child and lose my cool regularly. But I can also smile through a few more disasters every year and have found that practice makes patience!

# 14

# Coping With the Martyr Syndrome

Sometimes I feel as though everyone else in our family comes first! I can't sleep because the baby cries or one of the little boys wets and I have to change the boy and the bed. I can't eat because every time I open my mouth to put food in, someone needs a note for school, breaks a two-quart jug full of milk, wants a private consultation, or I get a call from the PTA.

I particularly remember a morning when I was determined to get to an aerobics class. It seemed that every time I had tried, something had always come up so that I couldn't get there. As I was getting ready this particular morning, two cute, preschool friends popped in for a visit. "Good, they can keep my little boys occupied while I get ready," I thought. No sooner had they settled down to play when one of the four-year-olds came with a plea for help to unsnap his pants so that he could go to the bathroom.

I hurriedly obliged and told him to use the upstairs bathroom because the downstairs bathroom sink was plugged—which Josh hadn't noticed as he brushed his teeth that morning—and there was water all over the downstairs bathroom floor.

I was trying to throw the dishes in the dishwasher before I left when I heard a scream from the bathroom: "Mrs. Eyre, Mrs. Eyre, the toilet's running over."

Instantly furious—not at the child, but at the toilet —I dashed in the bathroom and started madly mopping up the water with every towel I could get my hands on. I had, the day before, paid a plumber $70.00 to fix that toilet, which had run over so many times that it had ruined the ceiling in the bathroom below, which I had just paid a fortune for someone to replace.

I was making some progress when the other four-year-old came running up the stairs screaming, "They're spilling the beans! They're spilling the beans!"

Totally miffed, I stomped off to the storage room where I stood in the doorway to view two three-year-olds playing "singing in the rain," with 50 pounds of un-popped popcorn.

"Noah!" I shouted amidst their shrieks of laughter, at which time both of them jumped like popcorn!

The whole series of events was unbelievably pre-posterous! Needless to say, I never made it to my aerobics class. Another thing I wanted and needed to do was down the drain.

Even as I write this article I have stopped to change a diaper, retrieved the baby out of the china closet, found a pen for a six-year-old, answered the phone twice, solved three cases of sibling rivalry, admired Noah's "tree" which he had been "writing," answered the door, picked the baby up out of a puddle of milk on the kitchen table, and dragged two busy boys out of Daddy's den twice so he could write.

After such a day I wrote the following paragraph in my journal: "Charity (our baby) is four months old, and I'm feeling the Martyr Syndrome and that Fat Syndrome all at once. I'm definitely feeling like I'm not in charge. I can't exercise very well because of my back and ankle, still painful from the car accident this summer. I can't quit eating because I'm nursing the baby. I've been patient with being caught between a rock and a hard place until now. But I think I must just have hit the saturation point!"

All of the incidents I have described are part of what I call the mother's Martyr Syndrome. If we are not careful, we can convince ourselves that life is only a series of tribulations and vexations, adversities and ordeals, annoyances and plagues—usually suffered for a good cause! We can so easily become depressed and "witchy" and begin to think of life as unbearable and insufferable, unless we can keep the following four things in mind:

1. A certain amount of martyrdom is inevitable; it comes with the job.

2. Martyrdom can actually be good for you. It can be a way to offer anonymous service and to develop charity.

3. Part of the Martyrdom Syndrome is brought on by ourselves and our inability to get others to help. When you're feeling overwhelmed, tell your husband and children and outline some ways that they can help. Don't suffer silently! Put your foot down and demand some relief! Stop punishing your family by saying, "Never mind, I'll do it myself."

4. When a series of wild events occurs and you feel fully qualified to be a martyr, the overall effect is usually hysterical. Learn to laugh! Sometimes the humor

takes a little time to settle in. (The popcorn scene was funny almost immediately. We all ended up laughing uncontrollably.)

Martyrdom can make or break us. Sort out some possible solutions for relief, and laugh a little—or laugh a lot!

# 15

# *The Kid Is Always Right*

Not long ago I attended a seminar entitled "Executive Excellence." About 2,000 business executives in attendance were learning to improve their business skills, particularly in the area of management. Having decided that no one there could have a more difficult management job than I did, I went, not as a business executive, but as a mother. I was pleased and amused to find that almost everything that was said applied perfectly to my career as a mother.

Tom Peters, one of the speakers and author of *In Pursuit of Excellence,* was asked, "What about the old adage: The customer is always right? What do you do when the customer *is* wrong?" His snappy answer was a surprise to many in the audience. "The customer is *never* wrong! Neither party is right or wrong. You have to try to look at the problem through the other person's eyes. You will find that by looking at the problem from his perspective, although it may not be correct from your perspective, you can see why he thinks he is right."

"It's often hard to take," he admitted, "but a great manager can always say: 'I see your point. I understand what you mean. You're right. Let's work this out.' "

Too often, we become authoritarian parents who think we are always right. When it comes to a conflict, we don't bother to give the same courtesy to our children as we would to a brother or friend. If the child disagrees, he is almost always wrong! Right?

Just after school started this year, our eight-year-old son came to me dejected and forlorn, complaining that life was too hard for him!

"I have to practice the piano every day," he wailed, "and make my bed and clean my room and sweep the floor after breakfast and dinner! I can't keep this up. It's just too much!"

I giggled inwardly and tried not to let my smile over his misery show too much on the outside. "Jonah, that's not too much!" I began. "If you hurry, you can get all that done in a very short time and have the rest of the time for yourself."

But he had quit listening after the first sentence and was raving on about all the trials of his life, his hard work at school, his terrible Saturday chores, and especially this new added burden of practicing the piano each day.

I was beginning to feel a little annoyed at his ranting when suddenly something he said pushed a button in my memory. I remembered clearly one Saturday morning when my mother called me to get up and start my Saturday chores.

I remembered being bitterly disappointed that I was now old enough to help with the work and was beginning to be an older child. I reluctantly realized that my carefree days of babyhood and early childhood were over and that I might never get to sleep in on a Saturday morning again for the rest of my life!

I had not thought of that agonizing moment since it happened, but remembering it then made me much more sympathetic to Jonah's dilemma.

Suddenly I could see that what he was saying was absolutely true from his perspective. I was glad that I hadn't had a chance to express my worst thoughts which were: "Jonah, that is absolutely ridiculous! Compared to what I have to do every day, your plight is so tiny that it is not even worth mentioning! So many of your hours are wasted. It's so important to begin to learn responsibility. You're big enough to 'bite the bullet' on these things."

Instead I said, "Jonah, I know just how you feel." And I told him about my childhood experience. He smiled a little, and then I said, "Now you really are working lots harder this year. Let's see what we can do to make things simpler for you."

His heavy responsibilities really didn't change much, but he agreed that he could handle things by the end of our conversation. The most important thing to him was that he knew I thought he was right. Much of his burden was lifted by sympathy and understanding.

One afternoon when the children arrived home from school, an older child, anxious to celebrate because she had no homework, wanted to ride her bike with a friend down to a nearby shopping center. All it took was one child to mention the possibility, and there was a chorus of "Can I go, too?" One other child was already in the front yard with his friend, both on their bikes, so I said, "O.K. Shawni and Jonah, you take your friends, and go, and you other two stay home and babysit while I go take care of a neighbor. You two can go next time."

With hot, angry tears streaming down his face, Joshua complained of this injustice as I flew out the door, late for a meeting. I didn't have time for perspective or sympathy or understanding. When I got home Joshua's face was swollen and red from crying. I found that he had also worked hard to finish his homework because he had had big assignments coming up the rest of the week and that had been the only afternoon he could play with a friend.

I apologized for not having time to listen and tried to help him see things from my perspective. He tried to understand, but the fact remained that I had prioritized being on time for a meeting over his desperate (from his perspective) need to relax and be with a friend.

Such is life! Yet, I keep thinking that if I can just remember more often that "the kid is always right" (from his perspective), I can do a lot to settle conflicts in the home. After all, one conflict settled with sympathy and understanding out of every ten conflicts that occur is better than none, especially if we understand each child often enough to let him know that we really care.

# 16

# *Mothers Need Balance, Too!*

"This time will pass," an older mother said to me one afternoon when I looked as though I'd been through the wringer. "That's easy for you to say," I thought as I looked at her youngest child, a 16-year-old, pleasantly interacting with my 16-month-old on a windy day on the Boston Commons in 1971. "It may pass but 16 years is an eternity!" I thought. "I'm going to be changing diapers and cleaning up messes for at least 16 years—maybe 20!" (I did anticipate a large family.)

It had been a particularly grueling day, as I had had to carry a huge bundle of washing up 21 floors to the top of our apartment building to the coin-operated machine. I had had to stay and watch our laundry go through the cycles so that it wouldn't be stolen while trying to keep one-year-old Saren from climbing into the dryers and ruining the soap machines and trying to divert her attention from the candy machines.

Beginning to settle into my new life in Boston away from home and family, I had just come from my weekly grocery shopping trip where I was starting to recognize the strange labels on the packages of food more accurately so that I didn't have to take anything back when the total came to more than $12.00, my weekly food budget.

Although common sense should have told me that someday Richard would be out of school and be able to make some money, it seemed at that moment we would always be desperately poor. The week before my mother had sent a dollar bill in her letter to buy lettuce, and I cried!

I was teaching violin lessons two evenings a week at a home in a wealthy Boston suburb, and Richard was teaching driving lessons to a rich Iranian. Still we didn't have a lot of extra money when our one-room apartment cost a fortune to rent and we were living on student loans to cover the exorbitant tuition and book costs at the Harvard Business School. We rarely ate out and didn't have time or money to enjoy cultural events. My evenings were often spent alone while Richard studied at the library, or else were spent trying to keep our baby quiet while he studied at home.

It seemed that I spent all my time either trying to balance the demands of a very active baby and a struggling student-husband or trying to balance the checkbook by making money go further than it could.

I hadn't really thought much about those hard days lately until last month. I was in New York City and met a beautiful, young mother, with two children holding onto her skirt and a baby in arms.

"Tell me what to do," she asked desperately. "My

husband is in medical school. We live in a one-bedroom apartment, and my husband is almost never there because he is doing an internship. He's gone at least four nights per week. I take in two other children during the day to supplement our income until he finishes here next year."

Just as I was thinking that I would never complain again, she said, "The highlight of our week is Joy School (a mothers' preschool co-op), but some of the homes are so far away that it takes several transfers on buses to get my four-year-old there."

I shook my head in disbelief as I envisioned this valiant, young mother struggling to get those little children on and off busy, dirty New York buses just to get to Joy School. What an effort to balance not only money and time but also her own mental health!

I put my arm around her but could only comfort her by consoling her on her stamina and remarkable perseverance. I smiled, however, when I found myself saying the same thing my older friend had told me in Boston: "This time in your life may seem to go on forever, but in a few years it will be only a memory. Some days will be disastrous, but sometimes they make the best memories. Try to find some little thing to enjoy each day and learn to laugh at yourself."

As I think of each era of my life, I realize, as I'm sure you do, that there is a never-ending struggle for balance. Some days I can't believe I made it through the day, and other days I can't believe how fortunate I am to have so many children among whom I balance my time. The kind of balance changes, but the need for it always remains.

I heard a wonderful story about Renoir, the famous French impressionist painter. The artist Matisse, who was one of his best friends, came to watch him paint one day when both were in their later years. Matisse knew that Renoir had arthritis but had never witnessed the pain it brought to his dear friend with every stroke of his brush.

Finally he could stand it no longer and said to Renoir, "Why do you do this to yourself? Every stroke is so painful!"

Renoir looked up at his friend and replied without hesitation, "Because the pain passes, but the pleasure remains."

Each era of mothering has its challenges. Living with two, three or four preschoolers is one of the most difficult eras of mothering. Everything must be done by you—you can't set foot outside the door without the kids with you or a babysitter with them. By the end of the day you've picked up one-hundred-thousand things and are choking for adult conversation. When you move to the next era of mothering—the elementary age years—you realized that you now need to cope with self-esteem and homework and then those children become teenagers with their strong wills and emotionalism.

In a class on depression I once attended the teacher said, "I used to think that my life was miserable when I had lots of young children at home. Now I realize that those were the funnest years I ever lived!"

We need to sort out what needs balance during the mothering era we are living in and use a little more mental and physical energy in accomplishing that balance. In so doing may we all realize that if we can get our priorities straight—whether we be joyful mothers or witches at the moment—the pain will pass, but the pleasure will remain!

## 17

# On Time

What I thought was one of my greatest attributes has turned out to be one of my greatest faults, that is, my need to be on time. For years, despite my exhaustive efforts to herd everyone out the door early, I always ended up in a race to the car screaming, "Hurry, hurry, we're late." Inevitably somebody lost their shoes, sat in the mud, had to go to the bathroom, or forgot something critical just as we were dashing out the door.

"What about me really bothers you most?" I asked our two oldest girls. It didn't take either of them very long to answer. "Mom," they said sheepishly at first and then with more and more confidence, "when we're late for something, you can't get over it! You keep raving on about how late we are and how much we needed to be on time, but by then we're already late and we can't do a thing about it. We can't turn back the clock. If you could just quit worrying about it and just get us there, it would really be terrific!''

Observing myself during the next few weeks, I realized that they were exactly right! It was an obsession with me to be on time. Over and over again on Sunday I was saying things like, "Are you ready? Get your little brother ready. What are you doing in the bathroom so long? What are you going to do with your hair? How could you sleep so long? You always think there's more time than there is." By the time I got out the door, even after all the yelling, we were still late.

"Why didn't you hurry a little faster? I told you to get the diaper bag ready early this morning. You should always find your shoes on Saturday night!" I would rave on.

One Sunday I got smart. "We are walking out this door at 9:30 a.m.," I announced as soon as everyone was up. "If you're ready you can ride. If you're not, you'll have to walk. I suggest that you get ready by 9:00—but it's up to you. I'm not going to say any more about it!"

I stayed calm and proceeded to get myself ready and to help the little ones. Of the nine child-bodies at our house, three needed a little prodding, and six needed help with hair. I held a firm grip on my temper and at the appointed hour pleasantly told the two "fatalities" to hold hands and walk down the hill to the church. Amazingly, the next Sunday everyone was ready on time.

As much as I hate to admit it, I was one of the major problems in getting anywhere on time. As soon as I realized this, I began to discover "the speed of going slow." Somehow things seemed to happen easier, better. I realized that being on time is often at the expense of a relationship, and that is never right. When I hurry I often break things, wreck cars, and hurt feelings.

I am beginning to see that my rushing to prepare meals, to get kids to lessons on time, and being a little nasty on the way is never really worth it. I still feel the need to be on time and try as I might, I often can't help raising everybody's blood pressure in the process, but I realize how much more quickly I can actually get things done if I am calm and collected.

One Mother's Day the kids gave me a hand-drawn card with caricatures of each member of the family. Over each head was a little balloon which contained each person's most common saying. They could not limit themselves to one saying for me. There were four: "Where are your shoes?" "Where is my purse?" "Practice." and "Get in the car—we're late!"

I had a young mother explain her rebellious feelings as she was hurrying to prepare a quick meal. Arriving home late after running errands, she was greeted by a crying baby, starving children, and a husband who was supposed to be taking care of everything!

She related, "I was just feeling so 'used' as I struggled alone in the kitchen to meet everybody else's needs. Then my husband called me from the front yard."

"Hey Karen, come and see this beautiful storm coming in," he yelled.

That made her even madder. She said to herself, "Why do I always have to be the one with my nose to the grindstone? I don't have time to watch a storm come in. And he wouldn't ask if he knew about the storm that is going on in my head!"

But she stopped herself short and remembered that her relationship with her husband and her love for nature was much more important than having dinner on time. She felt her inner storm leave as that beautiful storm outside rolled in.

We do have to be realistic and realize that often the desire to be on time can have a negative effect on a a relationship with the person we are hurrying for, i.e., the boss, a friend, or a child. But the opening song in church can't wait until we finally get to church to lead it, nor can we let our children be perpetually late for school. Some facets of our lives require that we be on time. However, the challenge is to start using time as your servant instead of becoming its slave. Discover the speed of going slow!

# 18

# *Children Can Be Cruel*

Myriads of problems for children stem from the unkindness of their peers. These problems range from simple snubs to downright cruelty. There is hardly an adult or child who cannot remember at least one example of being hurt emotionally by peers.

A teenage girl gave a talk in church that has had a lasting impression on me. She spoke of how two of her friends had turned against her and hurt her both with words and by leaving her out of all they did. In this case, there was a good resolution to the problem as she learned to be more sensitive to others. However, sometimes these situations leave lasting scars.

What causes kids to be the gleeful torturer or the

snubber? The answer most of the time is their own insecurity! At first glance we think, "surely it is not the parents' fault." We would never teach our children to behave so rudely, even barbarically in some cases. But let's look inwardly again and think about what our child hears around the dinner table. Even the slightest suggestion of condemnation—"I don't know how they can live that way. Why can't they get their act together?"—translates in an immature child's or adolescent's mind into a perfect excuse to call others names or to look down on them because of what they are or are not.

Often our biggest failing as parents is not that we deliberately teach our children to torture others. It is simply that we do not teach them not to! Too often we do not let our children know how we feel about those who thoughtlessly hurt others. Many of these problems would be eliminated if we would express feelings openly when our children cause hurt or we see others being hurt.

Recently, our seventh grader came home deeply concerned because two of her friends had begun making fun of a spastic boy at school. When she saw them imitating him and calling him names, she was aghast! "Don't do that," she whispered as he disappeared, feeling hurt and embarrassed. After he had rounded the corner, she couldn't help asking her friends, "What if that were your brother or what if it were you! How would you feel?"

The girls, feeling guilty and cornered, proceeded to call our daughter names, making her feel as miserable as possible, and refused to eat with her in the lunchroom.

Of course, we were proud of her for her actions and retold the story at the dinner table, expressing our pride in her ability to be a leader for the right when it was difficult. At the same time, we asked if any of our family knew children who had been hurt or who were hurting others. We were amazed at the number of examples they cited that we were unaware of simply because we had never asked.

We carried the discussion one more step and asked our children if they could think of a time when they had helped someone who was being hurt or if they could think of someone to help now. The next day our seven-year-old wanted to take a gift with a little note saying she wanted to be her friend to a neighbor who, in her words, "nobody likes." Then the next day she invited another "left-out" friend to play at recess.

I wonder how many opportunities our children, especially our teenagers, have missed because I have neglected to teach them often enough how important it is to include others, especially those who seem sad or lonely. We don't teach our children to be insensitive and hurtful; we just don't teach them not to be that way or how to look for those who need help or what to do when they find them. They must be taught over and over, praised for their successes and reprimanded for their failures.

A week later, the same seventh-grade daughter was confronted by one of the same two friends who was having a fight with the other one. If we had not talked extensively about that young lady's correct decision to protect the handicapped boy at school and to always be kind to others, it would have been so easy for her to enjoy saying some nasty things about the same girl who had called her names. Instead, when the other girl said, "I can't stand Lucy, can you?" she smiled back and said, "Oh, I dunno, I think she's kind of nice."

The bottom line is simply this: Teaching children not to be cruel is not enough; we must also teach them and show them how to empathize, how to care, and how to love.*

The problem of what to do if your child is the one being persecuted also needs to be addressed:

Last year, one of our sons was the target of verbal

---

*For a book-length treatise of specific ideas for adolescent children, see *Teaching Children Charity* by Richard and Linda Eyre, Deseret Book, 1986.

abuse by three boys in his sixth-grade class. Predictably, these boys were the class bullies with problems of insecurity. Two of the boys got bored and quit after a while, but the last one got worse! When the abuse became physical, we decided it was time to do something about it.

I spoke to the teacher, who was amazed to hear that the problem had been going on for quite some time. "They only do it when she's out of the room," our son said, "or when she's not looking."

I talked to a good friend about the problem. Her son had also been a target several years earlier, a problem which had made almost two years of his life a bad memory. With a smile she said, "I wish I had done what another friend of mine did. When her boy was being tormented, she cornered the persecutor one day after school, and with a finger pointed directly at his nose said in a very straightforward way, 'If you bother my son just one more time, I'll break every bone in your body!' "

Although her threat worked immediately, I didn't feel that either Richard or I were quite the type for that, although I felt I could be pretty convincing.

After much discussion, we decided that it really wouldn't work to talk to the child's parents and might even make things worse if we talked to the child. As hard as it would be for our son, Richard decided to take him to the boy's home to have a face-to-face confrontation.

"Just tell him how it makes you feel," we said. (Although he claimed that he'd already tried that.) After many tears, he decided to go ahead and try again (thinking that anything was better than torture) with his dad standing by for support and with the boy's parents nearby.

When they pulled up to the house, the bully and his dad were just leaving for a karate lesson (of course). We had already discovered that this boy was an only child living with his mother and third step-father and, consequently, had a bulky set of problems of his own.

The two boys talked while Richard talked with

the parents, who were very supportive and understanding. When those boys parted, the persecution quit instantly and by the end of the year they were friends. I don't know that this would be the right solution in every case, but in this case we felt that our specific prayers for our son's welfare were answered.

# 19

# *Progression Through Adversity*

One year we started off our 4th of July with a big bang! I had allowed a young teenager to drive our van on a dirt road near Bear Lake while I fed our brand-new baby, Charity, in the center seat. Having never driven such a wide-bodied vehicle, she miscalculated as she came around a curve and hit a soft shoulder. We took a wild ride through a barbed wire fence, off a three-foot ledge, over a ditch, and into a bog. Without a seat belt, I hit the floor on the first of five or six floor-to-ceiling bumps. I managed to hang on to my precious, three-week-old bundle until the last bump. When we finally came to a stop, our 14-year-old daughter, who was in the passenger seat, turned around and screamed, "Charity,

Charity, where is Charity?" She was nowhere in sight. Still on the floor, I lifted up the flap of the captain's chair in front of me, and there she was, wrapped around the padded, carpeted pedestal, unhurt and calm as the summer's morning.

After I realized that Charity was all right, I became conscious of the young driver moaning, "Oh, I'm sorry, I'm so sorry. I'll never drive again. My dad is going to kill me, and everyone is going to be so mad!" My little three-year-old, who was unscratched, was patting me on the shoulder and trying to comfort my involuntary gasps for breath by saying, "Mom, it's just because we took the wrong road!"

I had a lot of time in the following six weeks to think about the lessons I learned from that experience as I waited for a compressed vertebrae, torn muscles in my back, and a broken ankle to mend.

As I lay in the hospital, I wrestled with the "If-only Syndrome." If only I had decided to wait a half hour to feed the baby! If only I had given our cute driver a few specific instructions on the hazards of driving a strange vehicle on a dirt road. If only I had hurried a little faster so that I could have driven along with Richard! (He had gone on ahead to register himself and the other children in the Bear Lake Fun Run, a nine-mile, traditional 4th of July race.) Both he and the ambulance (posted there to resuscitate heart attack and heat exhaustion victims) were called from the starting line to our aid.

For days I tortured myself thinking about the bodies flying around that van like salt in a salt shaker, totally out of control, and thought about how, at times, my whole life seems out of control. Before long, however, I realized that one of life's greatest gifts is to be able to overcome the If-only Syndrome by realizing that the past cannot be changed and that how well we can pick ourselves up, learn from our mistakes, and go on is all that really counts. It made me redouble my efforts to "practice what I preach" and dedicate more mental energy to balancing my life and to be a little less of a witch with my children so that at the end of my life I won't have to cope with the If-only Syndrome.

My second great lesson learned was one of gratitude! I was so grateful for a beautiful, healthy baby! I breathed out a silent prayer of "Thank you, thank you, thank you," every time I picked her up. One of the great blessings of gratitude is awareness. I became so much more aware of the great qualities of each of the children involved in the accident, Eli's smile and Shawni's compassion. I became more aware of everything—the love shown me by my darling mother who nursed me for days, and by my husband and mother-in-law who "hassled" the kids and loved them for me for weeks. And I was so grateful for two good arms and a right leg and a mind that still worked.

The third major lesson that I learned was a surprise. I found myself actually grateful for adversity! I had always wanted a broken leg so that I could have a good excuse to say "I can't" and here was my wish come true! Although it was a painful rest, it was really great to direct traffic from the couch for two weeks. I could tell each child as he/she took a turn how to clean up the kitchen my way and how to cook spaghetti and make cakes without my running off to a new distraction every minute. Everyone had to pitch in and help and learn new things.

I could fill ten more pages with the valuable things I learned from this small adversity, even beyond coping with the If-only Syndrome and being more grateful and aware. The most significant thing I discovered is that adversity is a growing experience if we let it be. It may sound crazy, but I advise taking the advice I chuckled at recently before I realized I would be taking it: "If life is just a bowl of cherries, hire a wolf to knock at your door."

# 20

# *The Early Bird Does Not Always Necessarily Get the Worm*

In 1987 we had the great opportunity to live in England for six months. I have the great blessing of being married to a writer, who can live anywhere, as long as they sell pens and paper.

In England the birds sing on the gloomy, rainy, early mornings almost as brightly as on the occasional sunny ones, while most of the households sleep. At 6:00 a.m. there is hardly anyone to enjoy their songs. Rarely is anyone jogging, playing tennis, golfing, or doing aerobics. Very few children are practicing as they would be in so many American households. The verdant green jungle of trees and bushes covered with flowers seems untouched, almost pristine, at that early hour, especially if you look up through the branches and not down through the silent rows of houses and empty, narrow roadways of our English country town just fifteen miles south of London.

Of course, many wonderful things happen in England...but not normally early in the morning. All schools for children of all ages begin near 9:00 a.m. Our lovely teenage neighbor, who is very intelligent and an accomplished pianist, gets up at 8:00 and is dressed in her school uniform and on her bicycle headed for school by 8:30. No school clubs or school athletics to worry about—only academics.

The high school age children are on bicycles or walking to the city bus stops about the same time and almost every mother walks her elementary age children (right up to 6th grade) to the school gates and waves goodbye to them as they file into their little school rooms at five minutes to nine. (These same mothers are there to escort their children home again at 3:30.)

Our American pattern of having the high school children out the door by 7:00 a.m. was suddenly given a six month reprieve. We began sleeping in until 7 o'clock and having a short devotional around the breakfast table before everyone went their separate ways.

That change made me think of other things that we could change. Our first impulse was to find Scout troops, music teachers, and soccer teams, but we gave it a second thought. We realized that these isolated six months were a perfect time to do some experimenting. We rented a piano and offered rewards for practicing and a home lesson once a week, but decided to let the kids take the initiative. Two practiced piano more than they ever had and the others dabbled now and then on their own initiative.

We had time to play string duets, trios, and quartets which we could not previously do because of heavy lesson demands. From our attendance at concerts and the children's exposure to music at school and musical friends, one child decided she really wanted to learn to play the viola and another the cello. Our oldest daughter found a wonderful harp teacher who lived closer to our English home than her regular teacher lived to our regular home— and took a few independent lessons.

I had wondered how life would seem without the hyperpressure to get kids to music lessons, basketball games, Cub Scouts, debate tournaments, dance classes, Courts of Honor, and "Tumbling for Tots." The answer was that it seemed wonderful!

Probably the greatest blessing of that whole experience was that I found myself with time to really *talk* to the children. Instead of being the presser, the task master, the chauffeur, the cook, I became a friend. We had time to sort out the inevitable problems of beginning school in the middle of the year in a foreign country along with traveling together on a one-on-one basis in the wonderful English countryside. The most important ingredient for any friendship is time, and I realized that for too long I hadn't had much time because I was so busy "doing" instead of "being."

With a little extra sleep, I also became a lot nicer. I actually put my witch's hat and broom away and only got them out in absolute emergencies—like visits from American friends and dinner guests.

We all learned an incredible amount during those six months. Once we got back, the children were quite excited to settle back down to the real world and the fall schedule with new interests and instruments. But I realized once again that the top of my list of my priorities with the children is always my relationship with them... individually. They may not be as far along musically and otherwise as they might have been; but so what! As important as I believe music and Scouting and basketball and dance are in a child's life, nothing is as important as your relationship with each child.

Yes indeed... getting up early is not everything!

# 21

# *Too Structured or Too Flexible*

Gail is one of the most entertaining people I know. I would call her extremely flexible. We first met in England at a tea and when she heard that I had nine children she warmly invited me to the second-hand children's clothing shop she was running two afternoons a week in her home. When I arrived at her compact house I found every corner, chair, and bedroom as well as a tiny garage-turned-shop filled with every conceivable size and color of used children's clothing and toys.

A young mother, the wife of a struggling medical student, was going through a pile of cute infant clothes for her new baby while her two other preschoolers were whooping over the toys. I decided that Gail was doing all this as a service. She couldn't have been making much money and whatever she did make certainly couldn't have been worth what she had to do to her house to earn it.

About a month later I got a call from Gail. I had mentioned earlier that I needed boys' Levis, and she had just received some. When I told her that I couldn't come on Tuesday or Thursday, she said, "I'll bring them over." In fifteen minutes two large plastic garbage bags were sitting in our entry way, filled with things for us to look over. The next morning after we had made our choices, I returned the leftovers and money at about 10:00 a.m. She answered the door in her bathrobe, bleary-eyed, obviously having just woke up.

"Would you believe that we're having a party here for 160 people in two hours?" she asked. "We have some friends who are moving to the Middle East and we thought we'd have a farewell party for them."

Baby clothes were piled on the piano and polo shirts for six-year-olds were heaped on the floor. A folded up playpen sat in the hall along with sundry other toys. While I made out the check in the tiny kitchen I met Gail's mother who was stirring a large pot on the stove and Gail's husband who came in with 50 pounds of hamburger which he said needed to be fried right away. In the meantime Gail wanted to know if I wanted to buy some apples which were leftovers from the neighborhood food co-op which she was also running.

"I order apples, oranges, cucumbers, tomatoes, cabbages, and whatever else is in season for anyone who orders them—about every ten days," she said.

The next week when Gail called to see if I needed any vegetables or shirts, she wanted to know if I knew anywhere a young Japanese couple could live for a while as house-sitters. She explained that she was a volunteer at the hospital, helping young interns and their families living abroad adjust to their new lifestyle. She said that if she couldn't find some place for this nice young couple, the wife was going to have to return to Japan for the duration of her husband's internship because their rent was exorbitant.

Every contact with Gail was similar. She was always loose, always easy-going and flexible, always helpful, and always apologizing for the mess and vowing to get herself organized and do better.

I have another friend who is also very interesting. I would call her extremely structured. Life begins for her at exactly 5:30 a.m. Everything in her house is numbered and in rows. Every child knows exactly where to put his coat, homework, and hair brush and has an exact practice time, which is ironclad. Her house is immaculate and her weekly menus are always posted on the wall. I know better than to call her to see if she wants to go to the zoo with us on Tuesday afternoon because I know that is her ironing time.

We are all partly structure and partly flexible, but we are usually more one way or the other. Think of your own personality and decide which one you tend to be on a day-to-day basis. Then try to balance your life a little better by consciously trying to be a little more structured if your flexibility is driving you crazy—or a little more flexible if you feel over-structured.

If you feel too structured, tell the kids to forget practicing because you're all going to the cemetery to put flowers on Grandpa's grave, or force yourself to leave the dishes in the sink and take your preschoolers to a park or forest they've never been to and let them explore.

If you feel too flexible, surprise yourself and everyone else by being on time for everything for one whole week no matter what kind of organization it takes to get you there. Organize the coat closet or get everything in the house put away at once and then have everyone take ten minutes to admire it.

You'll find that your life will be much more fulfilling as you try to balance structure and flexibility. I can almost guarantee that you'll discover some interesting and unexpected things about yourself.

22

# Learning to Praise
# Instead of Prod

While on our English adventure I had the rare opportunity to visit Scotland with three of our older children. In the short 48 hours we had there, we learned a great deal about Scotland—and about each other.

I was intensely interested to observe, even in that short amount of time, the fierce love the Scots have, not only for their own "clan" but for their country. Their pride showed everywhere; from the kilted bagpipers to the monuments dedicated to their favorite sons...Sir Walter Scott and David Livingston. We saw little old ladies practically swoon over the lilting lyrical melodies of Robert Burns, their beloved songwriter and poet at the King's Theater in Edinburgh.

The castle guides were full of glowing stories about their Robert the Bruce, their Bonnie Prince Charlie, and their Mary Queen of Scots, even though each of these historical characters were far from perfect.

Coming back to the present and my own little clan, I had envisioned two days of utter bliss without the distractions of the younger children and the baby (Richard was at home with the youngest six — claiming that he was having a wonderful time each time I called on the phone).

I realized right away that my bliss wasn't to be. The two younger ones were acting too silly for the oldest as soon as we pulled out of the train station. One child, who hates to eat breakfast, especially Scotish breakfast, became irritable before she finally found food that met her approval in the Scotch countryside. Another child always wandered off unannounced and wanted us to hurry through each castle and museum so that we could see everything. One wanted to spend all her time shopping and another wanted to spend all his time feeding the birds. There were squabbles about where we should stay and what we should eat and whining about things not being fair.

Just about the time I was ready to wish I hadn't come and give up the children as hopeless, I decided to take a lesson from the Scots. I'm sure there were always squabbles within each clan as well as between the clans of Scotland but they were always able to rise above them and show real pride in their clan and their heritage, forgetting the negative and dwelling on the positive. After trying in vain to change the children I decided it was time to change myself. I began to think about the good things that had happened. One child had skillfully navigated me through strange roads from the kingdom of Fife to Loch Lomond, with a map and a lot of patience. Another was always wanting to give money to the poor and disabled as well as to the street entertainers and was anxious to carry more than her share of bags when my load looked too heavy. The other was filling me in on English history to match up with the Scotish history we were learning.

I realized once again how easy it is to dwell on the negative and worry about things that are wrong about children rather than dwelling on the positive. Recommitting myself to letting these older children know how much I love them and appreciate their many good qualities, I began noticing precious moments I could have missed, including giggling outside the men's room door while listening to our 13-year-old sing to his heart's content in an empty bathroom. (His contented song, I think, was a direct result of my praise.)

I went home from that two-day adventure with a firm resolve to get out the family flag and rekindle a love for our family motto, slogan, and scripture as well as our family songs and traditions, to be more diligent in family prayers and to develop a real clan spirit for better *and* for worse.

Not only that, I decided that the next time I find my three- and five-year-olds not fighting, I'm going to tell them how much I appreciate how nicely they play together instead of telling them how angry I am when they do fight. My challenge to myself was to be more positive than negative, to praise instead of prod.

It's a daily struggle to look for good things, to tell children every day that we're proud of them and that there isn't anything they can't do. Sometimes it means biting your tongue and restraining your urge to talk about a child's annoying idiosyncrasies, especially if he's already aware of them. When asked what one thing in life he would do differently, the Duke of Wellington surprised everyone by referring not to mistakes made in any of his famous battles, but instead simply saying: "I would give more praise."

Sometimes it seems impossible to do, but I am convinced that if we can become skillful at dwelling on the positive and showing our fierce love for our children, not only will they swell with pride and confidence, but it will make a difference in the history of *our* clan!

# 23

# Give Yourself
# a Break

"What is wrong with me?" we ask ourselves when we see other smiling mothers around us, seemingly floating through their mothering career with children who have clean faces and seem to have never even stomped a foot in anger, while our own world is cluttered with junky closets and screaming kids. We see the "Sunday Smiles" of other families and long to be more like them.

Not long ago, I took care of a little two-year-old for my darling neighbor by whom I am astounded because she gets more done with three little childen than I ever could have dreamed of at her age. I had just spent a particularly grueling week with our constantly crying

15-month-old who was cutting five teeth at once and was dashing out the front door to the street every time someone left the door open for a split second (which occurred about 50 times a day). When she was locked in she spent all her time unloading drawers and putting the contents into the toilets.

Because of my recent hassles, I could not believe my two hours with this sweet, little charge from down the street. Every time I became concerned about her silence I would dash to the next room, only to find her playing with a little toy. We have never had a child who would play with toys for more than three minutes, but for her it wasn't just a fleeting thing. She played and played, all by herself, with never a complaint.

"No wonder her mother doesn't mind taking her shopping," I thought—a task which is at the top of my list of nightmares. When I take my two preschoolers shopping, the 15-month-old is out of the shopping basket in a twinkle, knocking cans off the shelf like towers of blocks and the four-year-old is off to find the lady who takes care of lost children because he loves to hear his name announced over the intercom.

I learned a long time ago to give very general and sparing advice to parents who ask for help with a personal problem concerning their home life. I like to conclude my advice with, "Remember, I'm not married to your husband and I don't have your children—spaced as they are in your family. I don't live in your house or have your mother-in-law"

Every mother's circumstances are different. One of my most admired friends has eleven children—all of whom are wonderful musicians. My head reels to even think about it until I remind myself that her husband gets the children up at 5:30 a.m. and sees that every bed is made and every child gets his job done and gets to his practicing.

So often we blame ourselves for the problems of

our children or husband when what we should do is realize that often they're just born with their problems. Some children are naturally quiet and obedient while others go through the terrible twos from about 14 months to 14 years. Some husbands are moody and hard to live with because that's the way their fathers were and they have never known anything different. Some children are born arguers and others are natural peacemakers.

One thing is certain: everyone has problems! The "Sunday Smiles" often cover myriads of heartaches and troubles. Some outwardly contented mothers who seem so unharried with their two children, aged 10 and five, are dying inside because they can't get pregnant or because their marriage is on the rocks.

We can take comfort and hope when we realize that the best person to help with our problems is ourselves. We are the only ones who are in our exact position. The hardest part of working out problems is using the mental energy it takes to solve them. Give yourself a break and instead of thinking of yourself as a failure, think of ways to get around difficulties that are put in your path. Try putting something down on paper next Sunday afternoon. Write the advantages or "pros" that you have to work with on one side of the paper and the disadvantages or "cons" on the other. Once you see both sides of your life on paper, it's much easier to come up with solutions. Use the pros to combat the cons. You'll find it interesting to see that some problems you have right now are only passing, and you will survive if you can just hang on.

Instead of comparing yourself with others and blaming yourself for the problems in your house, look at your list and realize that you're doing pretty well considering what you have to work with...in fact, you are probably doing *very* well...so well that you deserve to go out and buy yourself a new dress!

# 24

# *You Can Eat An Elephant*

Boy was I depressed! Every drawer I opened was a combination of junk and treasuries—all totally unrelated to each other. Five coats fell out of the hall closet each time it was opened. The curtain rod downstairs was broken and the new drapes torn by children whose philosophy for anything that is stuck is "use force." Two quarts of the dread, red Kool Aide had been spilled on our nice light beige, wool carpet and one of the couches was so beat-up that the kids were literally falling in and scraping their arms on the springs.

The children had managed to run the electric bill to astronomical heights even though most of the light bulbs were burned out. A great, gaping flap of wallpaper hung limply on the wall of the laundry room where one of the little boys had tried to build a tunnel for one of his trucks. We were tripping over the linoleum in several places in the kitchen where the seams were coming up due to the gallons of milk, juice, and punch that had been spilled over the years.

All the children were due to have their teeth checked and cleaned, which always ignited a rash of appointments to "fill the holes." Two children had teeth shooting out in every direction, one of which was being called "big teeth" by the kids at school. I was a year behind on the baby's vaccinations and the puppy needed shots. One child was saying that he couldn't see the blackboard from his desk.

Although my intentions were always brave and good for the children's practicing, it seemed that something was always coming up which made it impossible to get it done.

The food situation was pretty bleak, too. After priding myself on making something different for dinner every night for the first few years of my marriage, I was now beginning to wonder how long a body can survive on macaroni and cheese before it starts looking a little orange.

Finally one month I decided that it was time to pull myself up by the suspenders and do something about it. I remembered the principles we had taught the children one summer when we were trying to build a log cabin in the Oregon wilderness without the aid of any machinery or modern conveniences. We learned seven family principles that summer which we tried to put into children's language so they would "get it."

The principles included things like, "You can learn something from *everyone,* even if they're weird" and "You can eat an elephant if you just take one bite at a time."

That second principle seemed especially appropriate to raise me from my pit of depression as I realized that there must be a way out.

I decided to concentrate on one disaster at a time. For two weeks I did nothing but fix things that were broken, unorganized, ripped, torn, or malfunctioning and got rid of the things that were defunct in the house. That, along with a little new touch here and there, brought wild applause from my husband and children and sure enough, I began to feel better about my life.

The next two weeks I concentrated doggedly on the practicing. Right away the children realized that the old days of "I have to study with Judy for a big test tomorrow" were over unless the practicing was done first. By the end of the two weeks they were convinced that I really meant it when I said practicing came first— even before homework and friends. I was amazed to find that an actual regular schedule emerged from my concentrated watch dog efforts.

Next I tackled the medical problems—put two kids in braces and made appointments to have kids' permanent teeth coated with the new stuff that guarantees no cavities. The puppy and the baby got shots.

Then it was on to the food. For a week I made dinner in the morning when possible and actually planned meals for the whole week. Of course, I remembered that the reason I quit cooking was because of the wrinkled noses of the minority who always said that they didn't like anything but macaroni and cheese but that minority received no sympathy and soon realized that they would eat or starve.

Week by week, I worked my way through the other depressing items on my agenda, i.e. church responsibilities, PTA committees, watering the plants regularly, etc. and I was amazed at how much I could accomplish by concentrating on one thing at a time and selectively neglecting hundreds of other needs.

Of course, just as I ate the last bite of the elephant,

another one appeared and I realized that the house was crumbling again—BUT—it was encouraging to know that I'd done it once and I could do it again!

I also realized, however, that eating only elephant is as bad as eating only macaroni and cheese. Remember to spend a couple of weeks really concentrating on having fun with the kids. Spend quality time with your little ones and "sleep over" with the older kids in the family room after you've read to them from a wonderful book. Instead of thinking of your preschoolers as a constant nuisance at the grocery store, have them count the bananas (use grapes if you need more time) and point out textures and colors.

You could even spend a week doing things for yourself! Nothing tastes better after a load of elephant than a nice plate of fresh vegetables or a big, gooey sundae.

# 25

## Witch and Warlock
## (Wife and Husband)

Until about age six, our children have a family tradition of screaming when anything goes wrong or anyone gets hurt. Sometimes it carries through to even older children, but normally the screaming reflex subsides about then.

One particularly crazy morning, when three were squealing like police sirens at the same time, Richard looked at one and with a perfectly straight face said, "It must be something they're eating!"

Trying not to be offended by interpreting his statement to mean, "Could you please start feeding these children some healthy food and quit buying cookies!" I thought, "How dare he say that!" I had just spent considerable time that afternoon peeling and slicing carrots.

"It must be these carrots," I said wryly, pointing to them as I walked past.

With kids arguing and wailing about lost papers and shoes and a test they forgot about, I sensed the irritation in his voice when he said, "When is the car pool coming to pick up these kids? Aren't they late?"

Knowing that he just wanted them out of his hair, I replied in a low, even tone, "I am the car pool, and it's still a little early!"

There was not time for an argument on this one, but we must admit, after 17 years of marriage, that arguing is one of our favorite pastimes. Ever since our second date, we realized we each had iron wills, and of course, felt that we were always right. Richard is usually calm and rational, and I am emotional and irrational (and usually the one who is *really* right anyway).

The dictionary says that a warlock is the male equivalent of a witch. However, there are two definitions of a witch: (1) An ugly and ill-tempered old woman and (2) A bewitching or fascinating woman (or man in the case of a warlock). I definitely believe that I sometimes classify for the first definition and Richard usually fits better into the second one.

I find the way he makes beds fascinating. The agreement in our house is that the last one out of the bed makes it. But when Richard makes the bed, he can make it look as though someone is still in it.

The way he does the dishes also fascinates me. When we were first married, he insisted on doing the dishes on Sundays. It was a loving and noble gesture but after years of doing the dishes over again on Monday morning, I gently tried to dissuade him. "This is a family tradition!" he pronounced, "even in the old days before we had a dishwasher." When that convenience came along, I thought things would get better. But alas, every Monday morning the dishes come out with little bits of food plastered all over them like bugs on a car grill after a long, summer drive.

It was fascinating to me to find that Richard loves to eat a fourth meal every night at about 11:00 P.M., indiscriminately using up all the leftovers and messing up the kitchen. The biggest problem is that he likes to eat it in bed! "How can you make turkey casserole sound like celery!" I complain as I roll over with a groan, my stomach rumbling from my new diet. Smelling and hearing him eat is positively bewitching. To add to the joy, he likes to floss his teeth when finished! Clogging my ears just doesn't help a bit!

If there is such a thing as a child warlock, Richard would also classify. He doesn't like the rest of us to do anything without him. When I registered for a ballet class with our two teenage daughters, he thought he would like to join the class, too, much to the horror of the girls. He also has more strange ailments than all the kids put together. While claiming to have the body of an 18-year-old, hardly a week passes without a weird headache or side ache or debilitating ingrown toenail!

If someone were to ask if I still would have said yes when Richard asked me to marry him had I known about all these idiosyncrasies, as well as knowing that he would be late about 75 percent of the time, I may have thought 10 minutes longer, to decide—but the answer would still be the same.

For every weird thing I didn't know about Richard, there are 40 wonderful things that I couldn't have known in my wildest dreams. To name them would take too long; I'll reserve that for another book.

Almost every "witch" has a "warlock" to live with; yet I have a hunch that working out the differences will be one of the most challenging and exciting things we do in life, especially if we realize that the goal is not living happily ever after, but struggling and learning as we strive for real oneness in spite of our weaknesses!

# 26

# Witch and Werewolf (Mother and Teenager)

I had been counting the days until our oldest daughter could drive like a little child counts the days until Christmas. "At last I will have some relief in trying to get everybody where they're supposed to be," I thought.

The previous winter I had struggled with trying to be two places at the same time day after day as I escorted kids to 22 different activities during the week, including four boys' basketball schedules of two games each per week. "My day of salvation is at hand," I thought as our oldest finished her driver's training class and prepared to take her driver's test.

I was not prepared for what happened next.

"Mother-r-r-r! I am not going to wreck this car!"

this would-be driver exclaimed. "I positively cannot stand your gasping for breath one more time while I'm trying to parallel park. It makes me so, so-o-o-o nervous!"

She was due to take her driver's test in half an hour, and we were still ending up out in the road or stuck on the curb, or we were missing the car in front by only a hair as often as we were in the proper place.

Every suggestion was taken as a criticism. Once in a while on the busy city streets, when I had held my tongue as long as I could, I would yell—"Look out for that car!"—just in time. "I would probably have seen it," she would retort after screeching on her brakes to miss the oncoming car as she tried to make a left turn.

To my horror, I realized that she was a terrible driver! (I had forgotten all about the fact that I was a terrible driver at her age, too.) All my dreams of waving good-bye to her as she escorted children to lessons all afternoon while I read were replaced with visions of mangled fenders and prayers for "the other guy."

Get her license she did, however, and I consoled myself by thinking, "At least she can get herself to her own lessons and take herself to school functions." But even that turned into a nightmare. On the first few nights she was out late, I wrung my hands and listened for the phone to ring with a deep, somber voice at the other end saying, "There's been an accident." After her first wreck, my mind was comforted a bit by thinking that at least that was over!

As I waited for our two teenagers to return from a stomp one night, I remembered that I had wondered the same thing with each new age our children had progressed through. "I can handle these preschoolers okay, but what will I do with a nine-year-old?" I thought. When the nine-year-old seemed "normal for him," I began to wonder about junior high. What could I possibly say to an eighth grader? Just as that began to feel natural, suddenly I had to cope with actual teenagers, those people

who change from normal children to hairy monsters...
werewolves overnight. "How can I ever handle being the
mother of a teenager?" I wondered.

To my surprise, I found that teenagers are just as
different from one another as they were as children.
Some are serious and others silly; some gregarious, others
reclusive; most worry about themselves more than anything else. True, they do all have unpleasant scenes periodically and changing personalities, and they often
wonder how they ever deserved such a wicked witch
and wary warlock for parents.

If you can see beyond the present moment and for
the moon to set, however, and keep your sense of
humor, those teenagers become something wonderful. At
last we have the welcome opportunity to speak horizon-
tally instead of vertically to children; to really exchange
ideas with them about various subjects ranging from art
history to politics. We share wonderful moments, exchange funny stories about the "little kids," help each
other out of tight spots and fight over who gets to hold
the baby. Everyone knows that werewolves are really
good and kind people forced temporarily to be ugly and
wicked by the forces of nature at the rising of the
moon.

If we can keep ourselves from being the moon
figure during these times so as not to cause irreparable
damage, the light of day can bring "I'm sorry's," and "I
love you's" that are unforgettable. Those wonderful people become themselves again, full of adventure, love, and
fun.

After having lived 16 years with a baby in the
house, now we are embarking on another 16 with a
"werewolf" in the house. I think I might survive if I can
only keep mute during the "I-know-it-all" episodes and
keep smiling through such comments as: "Mother, things
are not the same as they were in the olden days when
you were a teenager;" "Mother, you don't describe my

date to the homecoming dance as 'a real cutie,' " and "Mother, you are so weird!"

Now that we're fully into the hard-core teenage years, I guess I'm going to live through the hand wringing, the fender benders, the declarations of defiance and despair, and the new-found friends ranging from tremendous to terrible. However, I am certain that I'll never survive being a grandmother!

# 27

# *Putting Excitement Into Your Life*

At first glance, it appears that Princess Diana has it made. After all, she married into the royal family, has elegant meals served to her three times a day, two darling little boys, a wardrobe that changes every week, a loving husband, and a friend-sister-in-law to share the excitement. On closer scrutiny, however, we realize that everyone, including Princess Diana, has her own cross to bear. Can you imagine the pressure of having to look perfect for every occasion, because the royal family is judged on your looks and behavior? How would it be to never have a kitchen of your own, to be followed by a bodyguard everywhere you went, and to have the press reporting your every move?

It is so easy to think that we are the only one with problems. Sometimes we feel that if only we had live-in help, it would be the solution to all our problems—until we realize that the live-in help needs help, which becomes another problem.

When we think, "No one will ever know what I'm going through," we are exactly right. Every mother's situation is very different! For some, the thorn in the side is rebellious children. For others it is indifferent husbands. For divorcees and widows, their challenge is having no husband or having an ex-husband who causes continual problems. Some have the tragedy of losing a child while others' chief trial is success. For many, the greatest trial is being too comfortable.

Not long ago Richard and I were talking to a man who said that his greatest trial in life is being married to a wife who is no longer exciting. "She keeps things clean and is a good cook, but everything is just the same every day. We never talk about current events or anything more exciting than her dad's garden and the kids' school activities."

Just as important as discovering that everyone has his own unique problems is the discovery that the solution to our own problems is change. Maybe instead of thinking how exciting it would be to be Princess Diana, we could think how exciting it would be to really change something that is making our own lives miserable. It's risky business to do so, and the only guarantee we have is that it will be difficult, the hardest work we'll ever do. If other people are the problem in our lives, we first have to come to grips with the fact that it is very difficult to change other people. The only person we can really change is ourselves.

One of my many faults is judging others. I complain about having to always be the referee in our household. Twenty times a day I have to judge who is "out" and who is "safe." Although I get it wrong half the time and throw up the "yellow flag" at the wrong time amidst the "boo's" of the kids involved, I guess I must like it because I keep doing it! I keep struggling to be the arbitrator, the moderator of the debate instead of the judge, but it is the hardest change I've ever tried to make.

It will probably take me another 20 years to completely change the fact that I love judging Richard. When he wants to do something that seems totally ridiculous to me, I know that things will always turn out better if I could say, "I'll do it that way if you feel really strongly about it, but this is the way I feel about it" and proceed to state my opinion. Instead, I usually make a quick judgment and blurt out, "That's the dumbest idea I've ever heard!"

Really changing things about ourselves that we know are wrong is exciting business. It involves lots of risks, which are sometimes scarier than cliff-climbing, but the result is progression, which is what life is all about!

Pick out something about yourself that you'd really like to change or that you really need to change whether you like it or not. Sit down and plan your process of change. Then work your plan. confide in someone else and ask them to check on you every day or every week to see how you're doing. Don't try to do it all at once; take one step at a time. Remember that you're in control of your life and that just as surely as your life is more difficult than anyone will ever know, it can also be more exciting than anyone could guess as you master self!''

# 28

# *Enjoying the Present—*
# *No Matter How*
# *Bad It Is!*

As mothers we need to realize that our day-to-day happiness depends on how well we can enjoy the present, even though the present may be difficult!

There is a routineness of life that is day-to-day reality for everyone, no matter how glamorous others' lives may seem. Because of this routineness, we need to keep reminding ourselves of how much fun we're having and remain positive about our trials.

It has been a year since I wrote the first chapter in this book. This year I've decided to quit hating Halloween, even though Halloween creates a mess from which it takes sometimes weeks to recover, especially when the "little angel" is acting like a "little devil." Although the altercations about how much candy to get and then how much to eat are endless, Halloween will happen every year whether I like it or not, so I might just as well concentrate on the good things. I've learned to love the moment when the three-year-old realizes that people are actually going to give him the world's greatest treasure, candy, and his mother was going to let him eat it (at least some of it). Watching the creativity of the children's ideas for new costumes was actually fun and funny this year.

I guess it's a sign of age to say that I have just realized that in only 15 years or so I'll be watching other mothers getting their children ready for Halloween and remembering the "good, old days" when I was racking my brain and searching the closets for costumes right up until the last child left the house for the last party.

In the future, probably one of our best family memories will be Mom and Dad's best plans to get rid of the Halloween candy by encouraging the children to go trick or treating early on Halloween night so that they could get back in time to give most of their candy to the trick or treaters who came to our house.

No matter what stage we are in life, we can enjoy the present, especially when we realize that the only constant thing about the present is that it will quickly become the past.

Gratitude can help us enjoy the present. We can even be grateful for depression (Chapter 6) and adversity (Chapter 19). Part of being happy, as naive and silly as it may sound, is being able to play the "glad game." Last week I was mad at the kids again for not doing things the first time they were asked. I went on a rampage and decided to do everything myself. However, I was careful to let them know I was doing their jobs. By the end of the day, I had picked up, hauled, moved, decluttered and organized at least 1500 things. My back was screaming as I changed and washed bedding on two beds, wet again by little boys. My split thumbs, acquired from too much con-

tact with cleaning liquids, throbbed in agony while I turned every one of 20 pairs of socks right side out and rolled
them up together in the laundry room. While in all that
pain, I remembered thinking, "Things must have been
worse than this in the Nazi concentration camps." Suddenly I felt a lot better.

We can also improve the present by "blooming
where we're planted." Just the other day I thought what I
wanted more than anything was for our house to be on a
five-acre lot in some secluded spot, with tons of trees, or
to have time to build a "dream house of our own." The
more I thought about it, the more I realized that I really
didn't want an enormous house payment hanging over us
for the rest of our lives nor was I willing to spend the full
time it takes to build a house at the expense of the
precious time I had with our children while they were
still each a full-time job in themselves.

I discovered that what I really needed was to quit
worrying about changing what I have and begin worrying about changing what I am. I needed to be dissatisfied
enough with my weaknesses (i.e., irritability and strong-
willedness to the point of obnoxiousness) to change, thus
making my present much happier.

In the future, the past always seems so fun and
funny, which is another reason to keep reminding ourselves during the present about how much fun we're having! If we can realize that most things will pass or change,
it puts them into perspective. Instead of worrying about
or being irritated that our 13-year-old's idea of great food
is Twinkies, Ding Dongs, and white bread with no crust
squashed up into a ball, I should realize that this, too, will
pass. I can hardly imagine her as a mother with her
future, little children following her around in the grocery
store pleading, "Please, Mom, no more Ding Dongs! Can
we just have some lettuce?"

The best suggestion I have to make your present
more memorable and much more significant as you look

back from the future is to have a family gathering each morning before the kids leave for school.

Even though you may hear a million excuses, this 15 minutes you spend together each school morning could be the single greatest thing you can do for your family. We suggest trying the following things while you're gathered:

1. *Read and discuss the scriptures for five or six minutes.* More time, of course, would be better, but even the busiest schedule can handle that.

2. *Spend five minutes memorizing a meaningful quote, sonnet, or scripture.* We usually work on one each week and give a special reward for those who learn it word perfect.

3. *Pray together.* Spend five minutes talking about the demands of that day, kids' tests, parents' meetings and appointments, grandparents' needs, etc. Then ask one of the children to pray for those particular people with those particular needs.

In 15 minutes you will have accomplished so many important things with your family. You have let them know that you value the scriptures greatly, have given them some memorized inspiration for times of need (of which there will be many), and you also will have felt real family unity in praying together with purpose and meaning.

The family gathering is not easy to do. We hold ours at a different time each school year according to the kids' schedules, and sometimes at different times during the week according to the schedule the night before. But those investments in time make a much more meaningful present as well as an invaluable contribution for family solidarity as we look back at them from the future.

The present may be hard, but doing just some little thing each day to make that day count, even if it's thinking about how "blessed" you are no matter how "unblessed" you feel, will lift your spirit and help you realize just how interesting life really is!

Even when things seem the worst, one of your devilish little angels pops up with something that helps you know that things aren't as bad as they seem. Just last week as I was leaving an aerobics class (which I promise myself to attend three times a week and end up struggling to at least twice a month) I looked back to see four-year-old Eli walking across the parking lot with Charity, his 18-month-old sister. For months he had been incessantly tormenting her, partially to punish her for taking his place as the baby of the family and partially to hear her scream. To my amazement, he had his arm tenderly wrapped around her shoulder. I smiled as I watched him safety maneuver her through the ice and snow. On approach he stopped, looked at me with a big grin and said, "Don't you wish you had a camera?"

# 29

# *Keep Looking Up*

Although I guess some mothers have survived mothering without outside help, I could certainly never survive without help from Heaven!

I attribute two things to any success I may have had as a mother and certainly to my sanity. The first is prayer. The most common admonition in the scriptures—to ask—is the one that is most easy to forget in our struggle to survive with our children until we are desperate or near tragedy.

Ask for the ability to see your children's little needs before they become big problems. Ask for specific insight on each child's concerns. Ask for ways to guide them in the paths of truth and righteousness. Ask for methods to help your children fulfill their destiny and He will show the way, but usually not without some pain and sorrow along with the joy and happiness.

Motherhood is truly a sacred calling, a magnificent refiner, a partnership with God. It has been said that mothering never ends, it just gets bigger. Through it all we learn to work with our witchhood, accept our weaknesses, and sometimes make them our strengths.

Some days I feel like I did recently on a rare skiing trip. With a friend, I wandered off on a trail which led to a slope I'd never seen. I was mortified when I looked down that Black Diamond Hill which looked like 200 yards straight down to me. Immediately I realized I was into something way over my head. After checking with several of the expert skiers passing by and being assured that there was no other way down, I took a deep breath, maneuvered two shaky turns, and then lost control and fell head first. After I had determined that I was going too fast to get my skis around in front of me without snapping a leg, that I was going faster than anything else on the hill, and that there was nobody in front of me, I decided to try to enjoy the journey. Like a human toboggan I flew, first on my back, then on my stomach with hands straight out in front of me and snow flying in my face. I whizzed down the hill totally out of control, wondering when and if I would ever stop.

My friend, who had not recognized me as I zoomed by, picked me up at the bottom of the hill and kind skiers who had seen the disaster brought me my poles, hat, and goggles which had been scattered along the way. We laughed with our husbands over my horror story at lunch. Although shaken and a little less confident, I did agree to ski one more hour before leaving. To my utter amazement, in trying to find the easiest way down on the last run, we found that same stupid hill! Absolutely terrified and with my heart in my feet, I negotiated four turns this time and then lost control again and went flying.

My friend stopped my whirlwind descent about half way down this time by falling in front of me to break my fall. Grateful but tired and weak I got up and fell again and again, all the way to the bottom. No one has ever been happier to get in a car than I was at the end of that day.

So go our lives as mothers. Almost daily, it seems, we are called on to negotiate crisis situations far beyond our ability to control. Life whizzes by with "snow" stinging our faces, and we become witches and fall again and again.

The important thing to remember, however, is that falling and failing is what life is all about. Becoming a good mother is not a destination. It is a journey. Enjoy the journey, relish the moment, put yourself into an eternal frame of reference and realize that time is just a moment. Know that the things that seem important are really only secondary to those special experiences and even those trials that our husband and children provide.

We must remember that there is always a friend in Heaven to break our fall, especially if we keep in touch.

Even though mothering is a universal experience, the second thing that I believe has contributed most to my mothering career is directed to those of us who are Christians. In developing this concept I would recommend an article entitled "With Your Face To The Son," written by Patricia T. Holland, originally delivered as the keynote address at the BYU Women's Conference on March 12, 1987 and later reprinted, in part, in the *Ensign* (LDS Church magazine) of September 1987.

Among many wonderful and inspired concepts dealing with women, this article also refers to one of my favorite scriptures in Luke 10:38-41. Here we read, in verse 40, "and Martha was cumbered about much serving." Although this scripture may have referred to the serving of food, or other services to make the guests comfortable, this line struck me like a bolt of lightning. I first read it at a time when I felt that my whole life was "cumbered about much serving." I felt that I was occupying all my time with serving my children and husband, serving as a PTA parent volunteer, a youth leader, a counselor, a chauffeur, a cook, a launderess, and feeling frustrated because there wasn't enough time to do it all well.

I read on to see if I could find an answer to my problem, which did indeed manifest itself in the following two verses where it says, "Martha, Martha, thou art careful and troubled about many things: but one thing is needful; and Mary (who, as we see in verse 38, had been sitting at the feet of Jesus listening to His words) hath chosen the good part."

I decided that I made a pretty good Martha, "careful and troubled about many things."

"But can it be true," I thought, "that in real life only one thing was needful, when there are eleven mouths to feed and six soccer practices and three soccer games to be played each week, and music recitals to prepare for? Could it be true?"

I decided to test Jesus' interesting statement on everyday life and found, to my amazement, that the answer was clear. As I reviewed the four gospels of the New Testament I read, "Blessed are the peacemakers," and decided that our house would be much more peaceful without the demands of the soccer season when we can never eat together during the week because of practices and nobody can do what they want or need to on Saturdays because of game schedules. After talking to the kids, we decided that our family would cancel spring soccer that year. We were amused to find that none of the kids really liked soccer that much anyway.

Music, on the other hand, we decided was something that would help us to follow Christ's advice in Matthew 5:16: "Let your light so shine before men, that they may see your good works and glorify your father which is in heaven."

Of course, every family's applications of the words

of Christ are very personal. Also there is a need for "a little Martha" in all of us. Yet, in reading the words of Christ and in growing in my love for Him, I realized that every problem I had could be solved through "listening to His words." Truly, only one thing is needful. Oh to choose "the good part!"

_30_

# _Time Out_

(Note: Saren says this chapter is boring, but for desperate mothers or even the moderately out-of-whack ones, I think it is the most valuable.)

While traveling on a national media tour set up by our New York publisher to introduce our new paperback editions of _Teaching Children Joy_ and _Teaching Children Responsibility_ to 26 American cities, I had the opportunity to talk to thousands of mothers from all walks of life. As one mother after another called in on television and radio talk shows, with problems concerning their children, I realized that most women who were unhappy at home with the children, (whether or not they had a job outside the home), felt that way because they lacked "the tools" of their profession.

Let's look at the career of mothering strictly from a business viewpoint for a few minutes. Most mothers have had other jobs in their life so we all know how scary the first day of a new job can be. Most of us can relate to the uneasy feeling of not knowing exactly what is expected or how the people around us will react to us. These feelings are not unlike those we feel when handed that first new baby to take home and "raise."

As our goals for progress in our new job and our list of expectations is defined, we're given "the tools" to help us accomplish the job. We become more and more comfortable with our position and it becomes fun as we do our best and make plans to improve our performance.

Not many assembly line jobs are fun! Jobs that require *thinking* on our part, creativity, long-range planning, systems to work out problems, and good co-ed companions are the ones that are challenging and rewarding. A job that makes a *real* contribution to society is probably the *best* and most fulfilling job.

Motherhood is the most challenging and yet the most rewarding career. Every mother has multiple careers—challenges in addition to caring for children. Whether the "other careers" include PTA, church work, community service, a part-time job, or corporate president, it is important to pull our minds into focus on a regular basis and realize that our children *are* our first priority and our most exciting and challenging career.

Our children are like fledgling companies—each struggling to get a good start. As the chairman of the board, we have to struggle and fight to help them reach their potential even though we don't exactly know what that new company will become and the far-reaching effects it will have on others.

Every hour invested with that company while it is young and impressionable is like an investment in pure gold—the returns are vast and immeasurable.

New companies are always difficult and hard to get over the bumps and struggles. And successful companies don't just happen—they are made. Careful planning, hundreds of hours of work and guidance, a vision of possibilities and tenacity are the right tools of success for fledglings.

All that sounds great but let's be realistic:

How do I really change things? How can I get a grip on my life when I'm hanging on for all I'm worth and I'm losing my hold? The answer is - you can't. Not unless you call a "time out" in the game of life and take a little time to see where you've been, assess where you are and determine how to make things better where you're going!

The first hard part of this process is getting away for a day to do some hard mental work. If you cannot find any way to get a whole day, one uninterrupted afternoon or morning will help. You can try anything from driving away in the car to a beautiful spot and thinking and visualizing and planning for a few hours to locking yourself up in a hotel room for two days and ordering in room service while you get your whole life revamped.

The second hard part is the mental energy it takes to think things through—to be able to see what you want and how to get it.

Here are some suggestions to spark your own ideas. Use the ones that can apply to your own situation and don't feel bad about throwing out the ones you don't like.

1. Write a statement of your purpose as a mother. What do your really want to accomplish for the future? What are your long-range goals for your lifetime? Think about your own needs first (for a change). What do you need physically, emotionally, socially, mentally and spiritually to accomplish your long-term goals? Set some specific goals in each area.

2. Determine that there are "seasons" in your life

that will require different things from you. After you have set some lifetime goals, decide what you need to accomplish in each season. Spend most of your time and energy in your present "season." This season for you may end when your youngest child enters school. Another season might begin when your youngest child leaves home. Still another may include a part or full-time job.

3. Begin to make your goals a little shorter-range by visualizing what you'd like to be like five years from now and write it down (i.e. more calm, more efficient, etc.). Then visualize what you'd like your relationship with your husband to be in five years and write it down. Do the same for each child, determining how old each will be in five years and the kind of relationship you would like to have with him by them.

4. Set some goals and ways to implement plans to become a better "partner." Think of your marriage as an exciting partnership that equally produces and shares the "profits." Commit yourself and your husband to weekly dates, and Sunday Planning Sessions when you can plan your week together. Try making time for a monthly five-facet review with your partner when you can discuss the five facets of each of your childrens' personalities (emotional, social, physical, mental and spiritual). Those of you without a spouse for whatever reason (and whose challenges are much more difficult than they would otherwise be), will need to adapt this idea to your own situation.

5. Determine to take time at least semi-annually to survey each child's progress. You can't plan what kind of individual he's going to be, but you can watch closely for gifts and interests and help him to develop them.

6. Each week, plan quality time with your children on an individual basis and collectively. You may only do one thing with one child and one thing with all the children per week, but those special times add up.

7. Have an "empty book" or notebook for each child where you periodically keep track of the special events in each child's life as well as the brilliant things they say. If you don't write it down, you'll forget it.

8. Determine to set family goals as a partnership and let the "fledglings" help by lending ideas. Establish yearly "majors" and "minors" that you are learning about together as a family. These could range from learning a foreign language to developing new friends to collectively learning to play tennis.

9. Decide to quit spending so much time "keeping score." Don't worry so much about whether or not your child gets better grades or plays a musical instrument as well as another as much as you worry about whether or not he is really being educated and how much music will improve the quality of his life. Worry more about your relationship with your child and how to enjoy the journey through life with him. Notice how often you "keep score" and quit it! It will make your life much more enjoyable.

10. Remember that mothering is HARD! Expect mistakes and failures. That's what progress is all about. Learn from the boo-hoos. Pick yourself up and go on!

11. Think of yourself as involved in the world's most challenging and rewarding career—mothering, and make it exciting and fun. After all, the bottom line in the mothering business is not just productivity and profit, it's people—little people—the future of America. You are actually shaping lives, breeding self confidence, discovering talent, and directing little people toward making contributions. You can do your part in a grassroots way to again strengthen the crumbling unit which is at the base of our national problems—the family.

After you've completed this very difficult assignment, allow yourself time to do nothing, or something you've always wanted to do but have never found the time for. Forget everything else and relax.

When you go home, your family may find you a different person. By experience, I know that I get much nicer when I'm gone (at least for a few hours). This precious time sprinkles me with Tinkerbell's fairy dust and suddenly I can put a lot of things into perspective. My husband seems wonderful (especially if he's the one who's been holding down the fort while I've been gone). The children become adorable and it seems exciting to go on with life.

I attribute any success I have ever had to these planning sessions. Although I don't fulfill all the goals I plan at these times, I am amazed that so many of them have come to pass, even though I have not done many of them consciously. In some cases, when I go back a year later to see what I wrote, I find many of the things I have accomplished—right there on my list! The mind is a wonderful machine. Once things have registered there and have been visualized as coming to pass, they often happen by remote control.

These visualizations do have a better chance for survival, however, if you spend a little time each year working out yearly goals, each month on monthly goals, and each week for things that need to happen day-to-day to make these lifetime goals come to pass.

Most of you will already have ways of planning on a day-by-day basis but try these two simple things to make each day more meaningful. First, before you write the list of things you have to do, put three lines at the top of your page. Here prioritize the three things that are most important for that day. On the top line put one thing you will do for yourself that day. (This could range from soaking in the tub to reading for 10 minutes.) The second line should contain one important thing you will do for your family that day. On the third line put the most important thing you can do in your household or at work that day (something like clean out that drawer or finish that memo). When your list of three is made at the top of the page, proceed to plan your day with the "have-to-do's." But remember that even if all you accomplish is those three top priorities, your day will have been a success. Those simple little priorities add up to real progress.

Next, balance your life a little by putting a line down the middle of the page of your daily plan. On the left side of the page put your daily plans. Leave the right side blank until you do your planning for the next day. At that time fill in the right side by listing the things that happened the day before that were spontaneous and unplanned. Be happy for those serendipity happenings whether they include a talk with a troubled child or meeting someone nice who helped you with a flat tire. Don't worry about the things that didn't get accomplished on your list. The happy accidents are probably much more valuable!*

Coming back to earth, we must realize that even with all that planning, there will still be times when we revert to witchhood. We will still judge harshly at times, and cackle when "Herman" falls over the bike you've told him to put away at least 40 times. But those times are the spice of life. If we can only have some visualization for what we want in life for ourselves, our husband, and our children, and have our own clumsy way of carrying out our plans, things can't be all bad. In fact, in many ways we will succeed in spite of ourselves.

Therefore...mothers unite! Take your career at home seriously and handle it as you would any important career. Never let it become an "assembly line job," putting the meals on the table routinely, chauffeuring, decluttering, making school lunches, refereeing arguments and feeling the boredom of routine. Instead, take the time you need to think and plan, struggle and strain, be creative and consistent.

*For more information read *Lifebalance* by Richard and Linda Eyre, Ballantine, 1988.

Like any career, mothering cannot be taken lightly. Being a good mother takes dedication and determination, patience and persistence, talent and tenacity, madness and mental energy, a sense of humor and sensitivity and lots of overtime.

The impact of our career is staggering. Good mothering can change the world at a grassroots level. Take the time necessary to think about it and plan it! Instead of filling the business of raising children with busyness, it makes sense to turn an old cliche around and "Don't just do something...sit there!"

# 31

# *On Changing and Not Changing*

Looking into a newborn baby's eyes is a profoundly moving experience for me. I can feel myself being sucked into eternity through those dark pools of light that glow from an intelligence so fresh from a Heavenly presence. (I can't help but think that these very wise, very old spirits must be very uncomfortable all squashed up inside of those tiny little bodies—no wonder they fuss.)

Sometimes I imagine that those tiny people keep talking to their friends on "the other side" as they giggle in their sleep and look past me to something I can't see. As time passes, however, they bring the present world into focus. Little hands pat, pat, pat everything in sight and grasp supporting fingers like gymnasts on the bars. Little feet do their clumsy tap dance and chubby toes and soles are tickled and squeezed by the hour. Little cheeks are kissed so many times that it seems they should wear away from sheer erosion. Little mouths taste, testing everything from funny looking toys to Daddy's chin.

Time passes, and things begin to change. Those eyes begin to see things differently. Sometimes they don't sleep long enough to let us get things done. As they get older, those eyes sleep too long when we'd rather that they were getting things done. They can't see why they should practice or why reading and writing are so important.

Those sweet, adorable hands drop sticky popsicle sticks on the carpet, write on the walls with crayons, and have even been known to hit siblings. Those same cuddly, little feet track mud and snow on the car seat that you have to sit on and often walk right into trouble. The same mouth that everything goes in also learns to make the strangest things come out—things like, "You must be the meanest Mom in the world," "This food is gross," and "Do I have to—like—go?"

But the babies are not the only ones who change. We change, too. We say strange things like, "Don't bother me," "I can't look right now," "Don't be so childish," and "Stop it!"

If we are not careful, we tend to start thinking of our children as a nuisance. "They always want to help with dinner or want to be entertained when I'm busy with a thousand other things," we think. Something always seems more pressing than reading a story to a preschooler or watching "Sesame Street" with them and talking about it.

I received a letter recently from a frustrated mother who had two preschoolers, ages three and one-half and one, and was running a small business via the telephone in her home. I thought she expressed many of our innermost feelings as she wrote:

"I realize that my number-one job is being a wife and mother, but that includes, as you well know, many other facets including cleaning, cooking, sewing, shopping, helping Dad, and organizing everyone else in the family. Sometimes I feel so guilty about not spending every moment with my children that I don't know what to do. I'm pretty organized and get my housework done quite fast, but it seems I always find something else to do and tend to tell the kids to play alone until I'm done.

"My questions: How much time do children of this age need to spend with their mother? How can I help them learn to entertain themselves when I need to get work done? Are my needs to have time to do my projects not important? How can I rearrange my priorities so I'm not neglecting my home nor my children nor my husband? I have heard women say, 'Our time to do things for ourselves is later when our children are grown.' As much as I love my children and want to make them happy and secure, I don't feel I need to entertain them 24 hours a day. Maybe I am selfish and if I am wrong here, please correct me."

Before I answer her question, let me say that the mothering years with two or more small children at home most of the day is one of the most difficult times in the mothering years. You have to do everything yourself. You can't step out the door without first finding a the mothering career. You have to do everything yourself. horrors) take them all with you. Mixed with the joy is a 24 hour a day, grueling job. People forget how difficult it is to get at-home work, church jobs and the grocery shopping done with two or three little ones in tow and sometimes ask you to do impossible things, which we often go ahead and do anyway.

Several years ago, I could have written a letter with those exact words. Though I still have preschoolers, I am also the mother of teenagers and an assortment of ages in between, and I can honestly see that I have changed!

I have always loved my trips to the hospital to have new babies and the ensuing rest—even though there is a considerable amount of body-reorganizing going on. When rooming-in was introduced in the maternity wards, the plan under which mothers were allowed to keep their babies in the room, I used to think the mothers were crazy who allowed their rest to be interrupted by the baby. "There'll be plenty of time for that," I thought. Now, I realize that I've someday got to come to the end of the new-baby era. I see how quickly the time has passed since our first new baby was born 17 years ago and realize that that child now has only one more year with us until she flies from the nest. Consequently, now when I go to the hospital I sit and drink in that lovely spiritual experience of holding that sweet bundle almost nonstop for the entire hospital stay. (For one thing, I know that I'll have to stand in line to hold him/her when I get home.) I enjoy every wiggle and grunt, every stretch and yawn because I know that tomorrow that child will be different, growing, changing.

I used to sit in Sunday School and die for the day when I could drop my baby off at the nursery so I could listen to the lesson. Now I find it's the most wonderful one hour of my week, just sitting there, she and I, enjoying each other's company. There used to be no end to my list of "ways to prop the bottle" or "methods to tape on the pacifier that really work." Now, nothing gives me more pleasure than dropping everything to sit down and feed the baby, whether she needs someone to hold the bottle or not.

So many other demands in our lives are screaming about how important they are, but I can honestly say that learning to eliminate unimportant tasks to do that which is really important has been one of my hardest learning experiences. I saw a cross-stitched sampler last week that made me smile. It said: "A spotless house is the sign of a wasted life."

Of course, some things must be done, but if you change the priorities of your inner mind enough to say to yourself, "Magnify the moment" and "Always choose the child," it really helps. I've had more fun tossing out so-called important things in the past couple of years than I thought imaginable. My husband, who is full of spontaneous delight, has even taught me how to leave a sink full of dishes to go splash with the kids in the rain. (He maintains that some people just don't have the sense to go out in the rain.)

Being realistic, we see that sometimes we need to choose between children. For example, two or three children may need you to be at different places at the same time—but things all seem to work out if the children see that they are truly your first priority.

In answer to the other question of the young mother: Sure, I still buy time with children's videos and sometimes neglect my husband. Some days I feel guilty when at the end of the day I've hardly had a moment to hold the baby. I do postpone things I'd like to do for a later time, but I also try to remember that nobody can get water from an empty well...that I need some time for me.

Even though through the years some things have truly changed in my thoughts and actions, rest assured that I still get out my cape and hat, broom and wart, and yell at the wrong kid at the wrong time because I'm tired and irritable and sick of the whining, weeping, and wailing that comes out of those sweet little mouths. Sometimes I feel like stomping on those growing-up, chubby little feet and shaking those stubborn little shoulders. Once in a while it's hard not to strangle when I grab a kid by the back of his neck and walk him to his room to sulk.

And even though I firmly believe that I should speak to my children exactly as I'd like them to speak to their children (which is exactly what will happen), I am thinking of buying them a black cape when they begin their own families.

Feistyness can sometimes be very constructive if kept in control. It helps children know exactly what you expect and when and just how much what you are saying means to you.

No, I didn't plan to be a witch, but sometimes our older children even go so far as to say that they think I look pretty good in black!

*32*

# *For Further Assistance*

HOMEBASE is an interactional organization of young parents which has the objective of assisting its members in becoming better parents, in enjoying their families more, and in balancing the various demands of their lives.

Four specific programs (each based on one of the Eyre's books) are available to parents through HOME-BASE:

1. "Joy School" or TCJ (Teaching Children Joy) is essentially a do-it-yourself preschool program where mothers form neighborhood preschool groups, rotating as teacher, meeting in their own homes two mornings a week. They receive detailed monthly lesson plans, tapes, and newsletters that focus on one type of joy each month and develop young children's social skills, self-esteem, and capacities for happiness.

2. TCR (Teaching Children Responsibility) is a program that assists parents in supplementing the education of their elementary age children. It takes place two evenings per week around the family dinner table and

turns dinner time into an exciting hour of communication and learning. Parents (through a monthly manual, newsletter, and audio tape) teach one form of responsibility to their children each month. The teaching methods and materials also supplement the children's education through simple exercises and verbal games on communication, creativity, and the type of learning that public schools leave out. It has been said that TCR teaches the "other three R's" of *responsibility, relationships,* and *right-brain learning.*

Both TCJ and TCR get parents more involved in their children's education, and both make teaching easy, because everything a parent needs (visuals, instructions, questions, and taped segments) are included in the programs. Costs to individual families are very modest since the programs are run as co-ops with tens of thousands of families sharing the costs.

3. TCS (Teaching Children Sensitivity) is a program designed for parents of teens and preteens who want monthly assistance in the goal of teaching (and learning) sensitivity.

Through TCS, parents receive a monthly tape (one side for parents, one side for adolescents) that discusses the skill that is emphasized that month (such as seeing, listening, empathizing). Also included each month are printed supplements and a monthly newsletter.

4. *Lifebalance* is a 10-unit audio tape and workbook program that helps busy parents develop *balance* in their lives between work, family and personal needs. It also deals with the balance between structure and spontaneity and between achievements and relationships.

Just by listening to the 10 tapes and filling in the workbook pages, parents can clarify their priorities and bring more *quality* and enjoyment into their lives.

To obtain further information about any of the four HOMEBASE programs, please call (801) 581-0112.